A Lawyer's Guide to Asset Protection Planning In California

Jacob Stein, Esq., LL.M.
Attorney At Law

A Lawyer's Guide to
Asset Protection Planning In California

ISBN 978-0-9839780-0-8

Published by Jacob Stein, Esq., LL.M.
Klueger & Stein, LLP
16000 Ventura Boulevard, Suite 1000
Encino, CA 91436
818-933-3838
www.assetprotectioncalifornia.org
www.maximumassetprotection.com

ACKNOWLEDGEMENT

I started out my legal career as a tax lawyer. I had never heard of "asset protection" until I met my law partner-to-be Robert F. Klueger. Bob is also a tax attorney, but he has been practicing asset protection for over 35 years. He is one of the first lawyers who saw asset protection as a stand-alone practice area.

I unwittingly followed Bob in his footsteps and never looked back. He has always been a fantastic source of wisdom and knowledge. His kindness shaped my law career, and for that I owe him a great deal of gratitude.

-Jacob Stein

TABLE OF CONTENTS

I. Introduction

A. About this Book

In our practice we routinely use several dozen asset protection structures. It is not possible to cover all of them in this book, nor is it necessary. Structures change all the time to take into account the changing legal landscape. To become a competent asset protection practitioner one needs to understand the fundamentals. This book will focus on some of the more fundamental planning doctrines and strategies and through them will illustrate the proper way to protect assets.

The reader will note this book places a great deal of emphasis on the practical implications of planning. We will venture well beyond the ivory tower and learn what happens in the real world. Pay particular attention to the chapter on fraudulent transfers. You will find it to be a very different take on this subject matter.

Every successful asset protection practitioner must have a deep knowledge of tax law, estate planning, business entities, collection remedies and real property law. Do not leave home without these.

The primary focus of this book is on asset protection planning in California. This means that we will focus on California law, but where appropriate, the laws of other often used asset protection jurisdictions (like Nevada, Delaware, Cook Islands, St. Vincent, Nevis) will also be discussed.

To make it easier to follow and find relevant sections this book has been constructed in an outline format.

If you have any questions, comments or suggestions, the author will be happy to hear them. You may email Jacob Stein directly at jacob@assetprotectioncalifornia.org.

B. What is Asset Protection?

For the past several years asset protection has been one of the fastest growing areas of law. In a recession money is scarcer, lenders are calling in personal guaranties, investors are suing promoters, and restaurants are defaulting on their leases. All these business owners and investors are clamoring to protect their net worth.

Asset protection is controversial—the goal of asset protection is to shield assets from the reach of creditors.

Asset protection should simply be about structuring the ownership of one's assets to safeguard them from risks. Many asset protection structures are commonly used business and estate planning tools, such as limited liability companies, family limited partnerships, trusts and the like. Properly implemented asset protection planning should be legal and ethical. It should not be based on hiding assets or on secrecy. It is not a means or an excuse to avoid or evade U. S. taxes.

There is no one "magic bullet" in asset protection. The term "asset protection" encompasses a number of planning and structuring mechanisms that may be implemented by a practitioner to minimize a client's exposure to risk. For each client the asset protection solution will be different, depending on **(i)** the identity of the debtor; **(ii)** the nature of the claim; **(iii)** the identity of the creditor; and **(iv)** the nature of the assets. These are four threshold factors that are either expressly or implicitly analyzed in each asset protection case. The analysis of these four factors determines what planning would be possible and effective for a specific client.

These four factors are not mere legal theory. We use them heavily in our practice to shape our plans.

C. Identity of the Debtor

In analyzing the identity of the debtor, practitioner should consider the following initial issues:

1. Is the debtor an individual or an entity?

a. If the debtor is an individual:

i. Does he or she have a spouse, and is the spouse also liable? For example, the spouse may be liable as a co-signor of a personal guarantee or as a co-owner of community property assets.

(a) If the spouse of the debtor is not liable, is it possible to enter into a transmutation agreement, transmuting the assets from community property to the respective separate property of each of the spouses?[1]

ii. Are the spouses engaged in activities that are equally likely to result in lawsuits, or is one spouse more likely to be sued than the other?

b. If the debtor is an entity:

i. Did an individual guarantee the entity's debt?

ii. How likely is it that the creditor will be able to pierce the corporate veil or otherwise get at the assets of the individual owners?

iii. Is there a statute that renders the individual personally liable for the obligations of the entity? For example, Section 6672 of the Internal Revenue Code of 1986, as amended (the "Code") renders those persons who are "responsible persons" liable for federal withholding taxes that were withheld but unpaid to the IRS.

c. What is client's risk adversity and budget?

You will often find that two clients in an identical situation will chose to pursue two different planning op-

---

[1] See California Family Code ("CFC") Section 850 for rules governing transmutation agreements and the discussion below (Section IV, Planning in the Context of Marriage).

tions. Each client is unique, and their emotions and character will greatly shape the planning.

Often, clients assume that if assets are placed within a limited liability entity, such assets are shielded from lawsuits. Another common assumption is that a lawsuit against such an entity cannot reach the owners of the entity. These assumptions are frequently erroneous (see Section VIII, Choice of Entity).

D. The Nature of the Claim

It is not sufficient to know the identity of the debtor. The practitioner will also need to know what type of a claim will be brought against the client. Here are some variables:

1. Are there any specific claims against the client, or is asset protection being undertaken as a result of a general fear of lawsuits and the desire to insulate the client from lawsuits?

2. Has the claim been reduced to a judgment? If the claim has been reduced to a judgment, what assets does the judgment encumber? For example, a lien will cover only those assets that are titled in the name of the defendant. If there is any variance, the judgment lien will not attach. Similarly, a notice for a debtor's examination will impose an automatic lien only on those assets which are titled in the name of the debtor.[2]

3. Has the claim matured to the extent that any transfer of assets will constitute a fraudulent transfer?

4. Is the claim brought against the debtor a tort claim? Tort claims are generally covered by liability insurance. To the extent that asset protection is desired, it is because the plaintiff will deem that the insurance coverage is not sufficient and will seek to get the defendant to contribute to a settlement with the defendant's own funds.

5. Certain debts are subject to pre-judgment attachment, if: **(i)** they arose in the context of the debtor's business, and **(ii)** the amount owed is readily ascertainable. In this case the plaintiff does not need to wait until he obtains a judgment in order to encumber the asset. However, the amount of the debt must be evident from the face of the instrument sued upon, such as a promissory note or a liquidated damage provision.[3]

6. An always relevant question is the dischargeability of the claim in bankruptcy. If the claim is dischargeable in bankruptcy, and the debtor's debts are exempt or otherwise unreachable, then asset protection planning may not be warranted—a bankruptcy discharging the claim will be sufficient.

---

[2] See California Code of Civil Procedure ("CCP") Section 697.910 (a).

[3] See, CCP Section 484.010(c) NOTE: Courts construe this statute strictly. The creditor must show that the debt arose out of the exact business that the debtor was engaged in. See, Nakasone v. Randall (1982) 129 Cal. App. 3d 757, 181 Cal. Rptr. 324.

a. The fact that a claim is dischargeable provides leverage when negotiating with creditors.

b. Asset protection planning and bankruptcy planning usually go hand-in-hand. Often the goal of asset protection planning is to structure the debtor's assets so that upon the filing of a bankruptcy the debtor's claims are discharged and assets are retained.

c. Certain debts, such as debts occasioned by fraud or breach of fiduciary duty, are not dischargeable in a Chapter 7 bankruptcy.[4] However, if the debtor qualifies under Chapter 13, even fraud claims may be effectively eliminated.

d. Federal income taxes are generally dischargeable in bankruptcy, provided that:[5]

> **i.** The tax is assessable;
>
> **ii.** The tax has been assessed or has been assessable for more than 240 days; and
>
> **iii.** More than three years have elapsed from the due date of a timely filed return, or more than two years from the date of a late filed return, whichever is later.[6]

---

[4] See, 11 U.S.C. Section 523.

[5] NOTE: This results only in the IRS losing its preference in bankruptcy. If the debtor has sufficient assets such that any unsecured creditor could recover in bankruptcy, the IRS will recover as well.

[6] See 11 U.S.C. Section 507.

e. California income taxes are dischargeable four years from the due date of the return. However, if the California tax arises out of a federal income tax liability, the California tax is not dischargeable until four years from the date of filing of the amended return reporting the tax that arose from the federal liability.

f. Federal and state employment tax liabilities are generally not dischargeable.

g. It is unclear whether sales tax liabilities are dischargeable.

7. What is the statute of limitations for bringing the claim?

a. The IRS may not assess any income tax after 3 years from the filing of the return.[7]

i. Exceptions: Fraud or unfiled return: no statute of limitations.[8]

ii. Where gross receipts (not income tax) is underreported by more than 25% of the amount required to be stated on the return: six year statute.[9]

b. The IRS has 10 years to collect any assessed tax. If the IRS cannot collect the tax within 10 years of assessment, the tax lien is removed and the tax debt extin-

---

[7] Code Section 6501(a).
[8] Code Sections 6501(c)(1) and (3).
[9] Code Section 6501(e)(1).

guished.[10] This is also true of assessments resulting from unpaid employment taxes.

c. There is no statute of limitations with respect to the collection of assessed California income or employment taxes.

8. What is the size of the potential claim? Creditors become more aggressive if the liability is greater. In addition, certain asset protection strategies are more expensive than others.

E. Identity of the Creditor

The third factor to be considered before implementing an asset protection strategy is the identity of the creditor. Here we are referring to certain creditor traits:

1. How aggressive/lazy is the creditor? How smart/knowledgeable is the creditor and the creditor's counsel? Accurately answering these questions will help us determine the scope of collection activities that the creditor is likely to engage in. This tells us how much protection the debtor requires. For example, there is a great deal of difference between a large bank pursuing a debtor on a loan default and a small bank. The small bank will often make for a much more aggressive and determined creditor.

2. Is the creditor a government agency? Taxing authority? Some government agencies possess powers of seizure that other government agencies do not. For example,

---

[10] See Code Section 6502(a)(1).

the Federal Trade Commission has the power to seize assets that it deems are used to defraud creditors.

a. The IRS is now prevented from levying upon any asset without first giving the taxpayer the right to a Collection Due Process hearing to determine whether the proposed seizure is proper and is not an abuse of discretion.[11]

b. There is no such prohibition on the ability of the California Franchise Tax Board to seize assets, but—as a matter of policy—the FTB will not seize a taxpayer's residence to pay a tax debt.

3. Is the potential creditor a spouse in a divorce that has not yet been filed? When a dissolution proceeding is commenced in California, an automatic freeze goes into effect, *i.e.* once the petition is filed, neither party to the proceeding has the right to transfer assets other than in the normal course of the marriage.

F. The Nature of the Assets

The final factor that needs to be analyzed is the nature of the assets we are seeking to protect. This factor, to a much greater extent than anything else, will determine what may be done and what needs to be done to protect the debtor:

1. To what extent are the assets exempt from the claims of creditors?

---

[11] See Code Section 6330.

a. The California Homestead Exemption ($75,000, $100,000 or $175,000 depending on the circumstances).[12]

b. Assets in a qualified plan, *i.e.* assets in a plan under the Employee Retirement Income Security Act of 1974 ("ERISA") are generally exempt from the claims of creditors.[13]

i. A statutory exception exists for divisions of property incident to a divorce. A spouse may obtain a Qualified Domestic Relations Order ("QDRO") which has the effect of requiring the trustee of the plan to disgorge assets to the other spouse pursuant to the order. The spouse may also reach the assets of the qualified plan to satisfy an alimony obligation or child support.

ii. Assets in a qualified plan that are maintained solely for "employee-owners," *i.e.* plans whose only participants are owners, do not qualify for the exemption.

iii. The Internal Revenue Service may generally reach the assets of a qualified retirement plan. In U. S. v. Sawaf, 74 F. 3d 119 (1996), the court held that the Service can enforce its

---

[12] See CCP Sections 704.720 and 704.730 and discussion below.

[13] See, Patterson v. Shumate, 112 S. Ct. 2242 (1992).

judgment by garnishment against the taxpayer's ERISA-qualified plan.

c. Assets in a non-qualified plan (called "private retirement plans" under California law) are exempt from the claims of creditors; and assets in an IRA or any other self-employed retirement plan are exempt to the extent the assets are necessary for the retirement needs of the debtor and the debtor's dependents.[14]

d. Face amount of life insurance and annuity policies is protected without a limitation, but loan values are protected only up to $9,700.[15]

e. Certain small exemptions are listed in the Code of Civil Procedure. This includes household furnishings, appliances and clothing (exempt without a limitation but to the extent ordinarily and reasonably necessary to the debtor),[16] jewelry, heirlooms and art (up to $6,075),[17] and tools of the trade (up to $6,075).[18]

---

[14] See CCP Section 704.115. "...exempt only to the extent necessary to provide for the support of the judgment debtor when the judgment debtor retires and for the support of the spouse and dependents of the judgment debtor, taking into account all resources that are likely to be available for the support of the judgment debtor when the judgment debtor retires."

[15] CCP Section 704.100.

[16] CCP Section 704.020(a).

[17] CCP Section 704.040.

[18] CCP Section 704.060(a).

2. How are the assets titled? If assets constitute community property, it is usually irrelevant that the assets are titled in the name of one spouse. The creditor can attach all of the community property, even if only one spouse is the debtor. This may hold true even if the debt arose prior to the marriage.[19]

3. The ability of a creditor to foreclose upon the assets of a trust of which the debtor is a beneficiary is governed by the Probate Code. As a general rule, a creditor has no right to attach the assets of a trust that is a spendthrift trust (but see discussion below).[20]

> **a.** Also, as a general rule, if a beneficiary has no right to receive assets from a trust (*i.e.* where the trustee has the discretion to withhold distributions or where the trustee has a limited power of appointment to choose among different beneficiaries) the beneficiary's creditors will have no greater rights to the trust's assets than the beneficiary does.
>
> **b.** A settlor in California cannot avoid his or her own creditors by placing the assets in a self-settled trust.[21] This rule does not obtain in many foreign jurisdictions that seek to at-

---

[19] See CCP Sections 695.020, 703.020 and 703.110.

[20] California Probate Code ("Probate Code") Section 15300. "Except as provided in Sections 15304 to 15307, inclusive, if the trust instrument provides that a beneficiary's interest in trust income is not subject to voluntary or involuntary transfer, the beneficiary's interest in income under the trust may not be transferred and is not subject to enforcement of a money judgment until paid to the beneficiary."

[21] Probate Code 15304(a).

tract trust assets, and has been repealed in Alaska, Delaware, Nevada, Rhode Island and several others.

Each of the issues presented above should be carefully considered by a practitioner before structuring and implementing an asset protection plan. The following discussion will address some specific issues present in asset protection in greater detail.

II. Collecting on Judgments

A. California Statutory Collection Laws

Asset protection planning is premised on the creditor's ability to collect. After all, if the creditor has no right or power to collect on a judgment, there is no need for protective planning. This section will assume that a creditor has obtained a judgment against the debtor. What now? What can the creditor do to enforce that judgment, to collect on that judgment?

California collection statutes—those statutes that set forth a creditor's collection rights and powers, and explain the collection process—are set forth in Title 9 of the CCP, entitled "Enforcement of Judgments."

CCP Section 695.010(a) provides that all property owned by the debtor, subject to certain exceptions, is subject to enforcement of a judgment. Community property owned by a debtor's spouse is included within the "all property owned by the debtor."[22]

Additional costs and interest may be added to the judgment. As money comes in from the debtor to the creditor, it is first applied to satisfy any additional costs and interest, and only then, the principal balance of the judgment.[23] Interest accrues only on the original amount of the judgment

---

[22] CCP Section 695.020(b).
[23] CCP Sections 695.210 and 695.221.

unless judgments are periodically re-recorded, in which case interest compounds.

Judgments continue to exist for 10 years from the date of the entry of the judgment.[24] Judgments may be renewed for additional terms of 10 years.[25]

Judgments are usually collected through the lien mechanism. The creditor will place a lien on the debtor's real and personal property (by recording the judgment with the county recorder's office or entering it with the Secretary of State), and the lien will be satisfied when the property is sold by the debtor or foreclosed upon by the creditor. Once the underlying judgment is satisfied, the lien must be released.[26]

A judgment lien on real property is created when the judgment is recorded in the county where the debtor owns real property.[27] The judgment must be recorded in each county where the creditor wishes to create a lien against the debtor. The judgment lien continues to exist for 10 years from the date of the judgment, unless it is renewed.[28]

A judgment lien on personal property is created when notice is filed with the California Secretary of State and continues for five years.[29]

In addition to collecting through the lien process, a creditor can collect through the writ of execution.[30] A writ of execution is issued by the clerk of the court where the cred-

---

[24] CCP Section 683.020.
[25] CCP Sections 683.110(a) and 683.120(b).
[26] CCP Section 697.050.
[27] CCP Section 697.310(a).
[28] CCP Section 697.310(b).
[29] CCP Section 697.510.
[30] CCP Sections 699.010 through 699.090.

itor obtained its judgment.[31] The writ of execution directs the county sheriff to secure the debtor's property in that county. Thus, the writ of execution is a levy. A separate writ of execution must be issued for each county where the creditor intends to levy on debtor's property. The writ of execution is effective for 180 days.

All property owned by the debtor that is subject to a judgment may be levied upon through the writ of execution process.[32] This includes real property, but the levy must first be recorded in the county where the real property is located.[33] There are several exceptions, which include the interest of a partner in a partnership or a member in a limited liability company, the loan value of a life insurance contract, and the interest of a beneficiary in a trust.[34]

Once the levied property is collected by the sheriff, whether real or personal, the property is sold at a foreclosure sale to the highest bidder, for cash or cashier's check.[35] For tax liens, the property cannot be sold until the bid amount exceeds the state tax lien on the property and the exemption amount for the claimed property. Once the property is sold at the foreclosure sale, the lien on such property is extinguished.

Following the foreclosure sale the sheriff remits the amount collected, less certain costs, to the creditor, unless the property was subject to other liens with a priority higher than the judgment creditor. In that case the creditors are

---

[31] CCP Section 699.510.
[32] CCP Section 699.710.
[33] CCP Section 700.015(a).
[34] CCP Section 699.720.
[35] CCP Section 701.510.

paid off in the order of their priority, and any amount left over is remitted to the debtor.[36] It is important to note that foreclosures of mortgages are subject to special rules.[37]

In some circumstances, the creditor may attempt to obtain a turnover order—a court order directing the debtor to turn its assets (usually a specific asset) over to the creditor. The turnover order is an exception to the writ of execution and is not easy to obtain.

B. Other Creditor Remedies

At any time while the creditor has a judgment outstanding against the debtor, the creditor may serve upon the debtor written interrogatories demanding information from the debtor which will assist the creditor in satisfying the judgment. Similarly, the creditor may demand documents and records from the debtor which will assist in satisfying the judgment.[38]

The creditor may also require the debtor to appear for a debtor exam before a court or a court appointed referee.[39] At a debtor exam, the debtor may be required to produce books and records, tax returns, financial information, witnesses and answer a battery of questions about past employment history, ownership and transfers of assets and any other information that would assist the creditor in locating debtor's assets.

---

[36] CCP Section 701.810.
[37] See CCP Sections 725a-730.5.
[38] CCP Sections 708.020 and 708.030.
[39] CCP Section 708.110.

The debtor exam is the primary reason why hiding assets and secrecy rarely works to protect assets. If the debtor relies on hiding assets, he would then have to perjure himself in a debtor exam for the "asset protection" to work.

If a creditor has a judgment against a partner in a partnership or a member of a limited liability company, the creditor can apply for a court order charging the interest of the partner/member in the entity.[40] (See discussion of charging orders, below.) Notice of the charging order must be given to all partners or all members of the entity.[41]

A creditor may also levy on the debtor's wages through the means of a wage garnishment.[42] The creditor cannot garnish the entire wage of the debtor. Pursuant to federal law, followed in California, the maximum the creditor can garnish is the lesser of: **(i)** 25% of the debtor's disposable earnings for the week, or **(ii)** the difference between **(a)** disposable earnings for the week, and **(b)** thirty times the federal minimum wage.[43] However, if the garnishment is to satisfy a support order, up to 50% of disposable earnings can be garnished.[44]

C. Exempt Property

Certain property of a debtor is exempt from collection by a creditor. The exemptions apply only to natural per-

---

[40] CCP Section 708.310.
[41] CCP Section 708.320.
[42] CCP Section 706.020-706.034.
[43] 15 U. S. C. 1673(a). The current federal minimum wage is $5.85 per hour. 29 U. S. C. 206(a)(1).
[44] 15 U. S. C. 1673(c).

sons, not to entities.[45] If spouses co-own property that is covered by an exemption, the spouses are entitled to one exemption amount; they are not allowed to double the exemption amount, regardless of how they own the property.[46]

For certain properties an exemption must be claimed by the debtor, for other, the exemption applies automatically. To claim an exemption, the debtor must claim the exemption with the sheriff that is attempting to levy on the debtor's property.

The following property is exempt:

a. $2,300 of equity in automobiles;[47]

b. Household furnishings, appliances, proprovisions, clothing, and other personal effects if ordinarily and reasonably necessary to,[48] and personally used by the debtor and members of the debtor's family at their principal residence;[49]

c. $6,075 of jewelry, heirlooms, and works of art;[50]

---

[45] CCP Section 703.020. This should be considered before a personal residence is transferred to a limited liability company, a limited partnership or an irrevocable trust.

[46] CCP Section 703.110.

[47] CCP Section 704.010.

[48] In determining whether an item is ordinarily and reasonably necessary, the court will take into account the extent to which the particular type of item is ordinarily found in a household, and whether the particular item has extraordinary value as compared to the value of items of the same type found in other households.

[49] CCP Section 704.020.

[50] CCP Section 704.040.

d. $6,075 of tools of trade, including equipment, vehicles, books and other (amount is doubled if spouse is engaged in the same business);[51]
e. $9,700 of loan value of life insurance or annuity policy (face amount is exempt without having to make a claim);[52]
f. Private retirement plans without a limitation, but IRAs and self-employed plans to the extent amount necessary to provide for the support of the debtor (discussed in more detail at the end of the outline);[53] and
g. Certain claims for unemployment insurance, personal injury or workers insurance (without making a claim for exemption).

In addition to the above property, real property may be exempt to the extent the debtor has a homestead in the real property. Homestead real property is property which is the debtor's principal residence in which the debtor is residing at the time of the judgment and at the time of the collection. Homestead covers houses, condominiums, mobile homes, boats and other abodes of the debtor.[54]

The exempt amount of a homestead property is: **(i)** $75,000 unless clauses **(ii)** or **(iii)** apply; **(ii)** $100,000 if someone other than a debtor resides on the property and

---

[51] CCP Section 704.060.
[52] CCP Section 704.100.
[53] CCP Section 704.115.
[54] CCP Section 704.710.

that other person does not have an ownership interest in the property, other than as a community property interest; or **(iii)** $175,000 for those debtors who are over 65 or physically disabled.[55] Spouses are not allowed to double their homestead exemption.[56]

A court order is required for the sale of the property in which a debtor has a homestead. Consequently, a debtor is not required to file a homestead declaration to benefit from the homestead exemption. However, a homestead declaration may be filed to designate a specific property as a homestead when two or more properties can be treated as the debtor's primary residence.

D. Exemption Planning

Exemption planning can be an important aspect of asset protection. Even if bankruptcy is contemplated, as discussed below, the debtor is allowed a choice of the exemptions provided by his or her state of residency and the bankruptcy code.[57] To be able to use a state's exemption statutes in the bankruptcy context, the debtor must have been domiciled in such state for at least 180 days. To be able to use an exemption for non-bankruptcy purposes, some states require residency, while others don't. This means that with respect to exemption planning, debtors

---

[55] CCP Section 704.730(a).

[56] CCP Section 704.730(b).

[57] Some states, including California, have opted out of this choice, which means that debtors in these states can only use the state's exemptions.

have an ability to shop for states with the best exemption scheme.

The three most significant exemptions are the homestead, life insurance and retirement plan exemptions.

Generally, a homestead exemption means that a creditor cannot force the sale of a property where the equity is protected by the homestead, and if the debtor sells the property, the sale proceeds are protected to the extent of the homestead.

In many states the homestead exemption greatly exceeds all other available exemptions. In California the homestead exemption can be $75,000, $100,000 or $175,000, with most debtors falling in the $100,000 range. While this exemption is generous compared to many other states, some states allow an even greater exemption.

For example, Arizona and Massachusetts allow a flat $100,000 exemption, while Minnesota allows a $200,000 exemption.[58] In Kansas, the exemption is unlimited for city lots not exceeding one acre (except for tax liabilities).[59]

The constitutions of Florida and Texas provide for unlimited homestead exemptions, although the size of the land is limited (Florida: 160 acres of rural land, and one-half acre of city land; Texas: 200 acres of rural land and 10 acres of city land).[60]

It is important to remember that despite the amount of the homestead exemption, it does not exempt claims of all

---

[58] Ariz. Rev. Statutes Section 33-1101(A) and (B); Mass. Gen. Laws ch. 188, Section 1; Minn. Stat. Section 510.02.

[59] Kan. Stat. Annotated Section 60-2301.

[60] Fla. Const. Article X, Section 4(a)(1); Tex. Const. Article XVI, Section 51.

creditors. Certain creditors are not impacted by the homestead: the federal[61] and state governments for tax claims; alimony and child support claims; purchase money creditors who usually retain a security interest in the property; and debts for the improvement of the subject property.

In addition to the homestead exemption, many states grant a large exemption for life insurance. In California, there is no limitation on the face amount of insurance protected, but there is a $9,700 limitation on cash surrender value. In several states there is no limitation on protection afforded to cash surrender value. For example, in Florida cash surrender value is protected without a limit if the policy is owned by a state resident.[62]

The exemption afforded to retirement plans is so significant that an entire chapter of the book is devoted to it.

---

[61] The Service is allowed to force the sale of property to satisfy tax claims under Code Sections 6321 and 6331.

[62] Fla. Stat. Annotated Section 222.14.

III. Fraudulent Transfers

A. Introduction

The modern American law governing fraudulent conveyances has its origins in the Statute of Elizabeth, originally codified in the 16th century England—13 Eliz. Ch. 5 (1571). The original penalty under the Statute of Elizabeth was the forfeiture of the property's value, half to the royal treasury and half to the creditor. Most English common law jurisdictions have adopted the Statute of Elizabeth in some form.

The Uniform Fraudulent Conveyance Act of 1918 was the first codification of the Statute of Elizabeth in the United States and was adopted by 26 jurisdictions. A more modern adaptation of that act is the Uniform Fraudulent Transfer Act (the "UFTA") adopted by California as of January 1, 1987.

The fraudulent transfer laws may apply and must be considered in connection with any transfer that diminishes the value of property owned by the debtor: transfers to family members, partnerships, trusts, corporations and others.

If the transfer is fraudulent, the creditors remedy, generally, is to set aside the transfer and proceed after the transferee. In certain cases, the court may even grant to the creditor injunctive relief (including pre-judgment) to prevent any further transfers. In the context of bankruptcy, a fraudulent transfer allows the creditor to avoid such transfer and can result in denial of relief to the debtor.

It is important to note that the fraudulent transfer laws will apply only to transfers of property in which the debtor holds a beneficial interest. This means that if the debtor simply holds legal title in the property (such as when property is retitled to facilitate a loan), the transfer of such property cannot be set aside by a creditor.

Despite a common misconception, it is important to remember that a fraudulent transfer is not fraud. Fraud usually involves lying: "a knowing misrepresentation of the truth or concealment of a material fact to induce another to act to his or her detriment."[63] Thus, a used car dealer rolling back the odometer is committing an act of fraud. A plaintiff who proves fraud by the defendant is entitled to damages, including, possibly, punitive damages.

Unlike fraud, fraudulent transfers do not require a finding of fraud. As discussed below, a transfer maybe fraudulent without a finding of any ill intent on behalf of the debtor. Fraudulent transfers are valid transfers, but, as discussed below, may be voided by a creditor. This means that a fraudulent transfer of property is good for all legal purposes, except as to a creditor.

B. Current Law in California

1. UFTA

The UFTA is contained in the California Civil Code ("CCC") Sections 3439-3439.12. There are two types of fraudulent transfers. Those made with actual intent to de-

---

[63] Black's Law Dictionary, 670-671 (7th ed. 1999).

fraud a creditor—here we are looking at the debtor's motivation for engaging in the transfer. CCC Section 3439.04 defines this type of fraudulent transfer as:

> **A transfer made** or obligation incurred by a debtor is **fraudulent** as to a creditor, whether the creditor's claim arose before or after the transfer was made or the obligation was incurred, **if the debtor made the transfer** or incurred the obligation as follows:
>
> **(a)** With **actual intent to hinder, delay, or defraud** any creditor of the debtor.
> **(b)** Without receiving a reasonably **equivalent value in exchange** for the transfer or obligation, and the debtor:
>
> > **(1)** Was engaged or was about to engage in a business or a transaction for which the remaining assets of the debtor were unreasonably small in relation to the business or transaction; or
> > **(2)** Intended to incur, or believed, or reasonably should have believed, that he or she would incur debts beyond his or her ability to pay as they became due.
>
> (Emphasis added.)

The other type of a fraudulent transfer is one where the transfer is in essence a gift, and the debtor is insolvent. Here, the debtor's intent is irrelevant and the transfer is called constructively fraudulent. CCC Section 3439.05 provides:

> A **transfer made** or obligation incurred by a debtor is fraudulent as to a creditor whose **claim arose before the transfer** was made or the obligation was incurred if the debtor made the transfer or incurred the obligation without receiving a **reasonably equivalent value in exchange** for the transfer or obligation and the **debtor was insolvent** at that time or the **debtor became insolvent** as a result of the transfer or obligation. (Emphasis added.)

The creditor has a limited amount of time to bring a fraudulent transfer action. CCC Section 3439.09 provides in part:

> A cause of action with respect to a fraudulent transfer…is extinguished unless action is brought…
>
>> **(a)** Under subdivision (a) of Section 3439.04 [intent to hinder, delay, defraud], within **four years after the transfer was made**... or, if later, within **one year** after the transfer…could reasonably have been **discovered by the claimant**.
>> **(b)** Under subdivision (b) of Section 3439.04 or Section 3439.05 [equivalent value not received in return for transfer], within **four years** after the transfer was made…
>> **(c)** Notwithstanding any other provision of law, a cause of action with respect to a fraudulent transfer or obligation is **extin-**

guished if no action is brought or levy made within **seven years** after the transfer was made or the obligation was incurred.

2. Transfers

A conveyance of property by a debtor will be treated as a "transfer" for fraudulent transfer purposes if such conveyance diminishes the value of debtor's property.[64] This means that if the debtor conveys fully encumbered property (*i.e.*, property with no equity), that will not be treated as a transfer.[65] Similarly, if the transferred property is covered by an available exemption, that cannot be a fraudulent transfer because it does not diminish what the creditor may receive.[66]

The California Civil Code defines the term "transfer" as every mode, direct or indirect, absolute or conditional, voluntary or involuntary, of disposing of or parting with an asset or an interest in an asset, and includes payment of money, release, lease, and creation of a lien or other encumbrance.[67]

In addition to transactions that are transfers on their face, certain other events may be treated as transfers: inac-

---

[64] Collier on Bankruptcy (15th ed. 1993).

[65] CCC Section 3439.01(a)(1). Mehrtash v. ATA Mehrtash, 93 Cal. App. 4th 75 (2001) (the transfer of real property subject to encumbrances, including judgment liens, could not be set aside as a fraudulent transfer, as the creditor could not show how she was injured).

[66] CCC Section 3439.01(a)(2). Reddy v. Gonzalez, 8 Cal. App. 4th 118, 122 (1992) (homestead property not subject to fraudulent transfer laws).

[67] CCC Section 3439.01(i).

tion, a waiver of defenses, the termination of a lease, an extension of a loan, a disclaimer, making a tax election, withdrawing cash from a deposit account, granting a security interest in property, conversion of nonexempt assets into exempt assets (even though the transaction can be characterized as a debtor transferring assets to herself), perfecting a security interest or obtaining a lien, and rental of property for less than fair market value.

Just as it is important to know what would constitute a transfer, it is equally important to know what would not be a transfer: a clerical action (like retitling property to correct title), a transfer (by operation of law) by someone other than the debtor, or a mandatory (by operation of law) transfer by the debtor. For example, a transfer of assets to an ex-spouse pursuant to a divorce decree does not constitute an avoidable transfer.

Additionally, indirect transfers are not treated as transfers. For example, a transfer by a corporation controlled by a debtor is not treated as a transfer being made by the debtor.

In a transaction where the debtor acquires an asset or sells an asset, the transfer takes place when the obligation to pay consideration arises. Thus, on a transfer of land for a promissory note, the transfer for UFTA purposes takes place when the first installment is due on the note.[68] The timing of the transfer may be of crucial importance, as it

---

[68] For bankruptcy law purposes, a transfer (for fraudulent transfer purposes only) will take place when the title in the transferred property is perfected in such a way that no one would be able to acquire title in the property superior to that of the transferee.

determines the value of the transferred property and must also coincide with intent to defraud.

3. Types of Fraud

As CCC Sections 3439.04(a) and (b) demonstrate, there are two types of fraudulent transfers: those done with an actual intent to defraud, delay or hinder a creditor, and those done for less than full consideration while the debtor was insolvent (constructive fraud).

a. Actual Intent

i. Looking for Intent

A transfer will be fraudulent if made with **actual intent** to hinder, delay or defraud any creditor.[69] Thus, if a transfer is made with the specific intent to avoid satisfying a specific liability, then actual intent is present. However, when a debtor prefers to pay one creditor instead of another, that is not a fraudulent transfer.[70] For these types of fraudulent transfers, the transferor's intent is the primary factor.

Actual intent focuses on the mindset of the debtor at the time of the transfer. Regardless of the financial situation of the debtor, or the amount of the consideration received by

---

[69] CCC Section 3439.04(a). One should remember, that while the intent to defraud is usually the issue, a transaction can also be set aside for intent to delay or hinder, such as a contribution of assets to a partnership or a corporation.
[70] CCC Section 3432.

the creditor, a showing of actual intent to defraud can be used to set aside any transfer.

One of the most important principles of asset protection planning is acting while the seas are calm. The importance of that principle is clearly evident in light of the actual intent test. The actual intent test requires the existence of a connection between the debtor and the creditor at the time of the transfer. If a debtor transfers assets when he or she has no creditors, then the debtor will obviously lack the requisite actual intent to defraud some specific person.

ii. Badges of Fraud

Evidence of actual intent is rarely available to a creditor, for it would require proof of someone's inner thoughts. Because of that, creditors often have to rely on circumstantial evidence of fraud. To prove actual intent, the courts have developed "*badges of fraud*," which, while not conclusive, are considered by the courts as circumstantial evidence of fraud. The ten badges of fraud are:

1. Becoming insolvent because of the transfer;
2. Lack or inadequacy of consideration;
3. Family, or insider relationship among parties;
4. The retention of possession, benefits or use of property in question;
5. The existence of the threat of litigation;
6. The financial situation of the debtor at the time of transfer or after transfer;
7. The existence or a cumulative effect of a series of transactions after the onset of debtor's financial difficulties;

8. The general chronology of events;
9. The secrecy of the transaction in question; and
10. Deviation from the usual method or course of business.

The presence of one or more badges of fraud will serve to shift the burden of proof from the creditor to the debtor. Thus, at the outset the creditor is settled with the responsibility of establishing existence of this circumstantial evidence. When that is successfully accomplished, the debtor must then prove that despite this circumstantial evidence, the transfer was made with no fraudulent intent.

Badges of fraud were originally developed by the common-law English courts. The same principles continue to apply today, and there is a mounting body of case law on the subject. Based on these cases, the asset protection adviser should keep in mind the following pointers:

- Asset protection planning should not be secretive, or concealed. It should be open and recorded if involving real property.
- Transfers of assets should be accomplished at arm's length, following customary business practices, and should be papered like any other business transaction.
- Transfers to related parties, whether family members or controlled entities are always suspect and scrutinized more closely by the courts.
- Transfers should be made for adequate consideration, and, if possible, the sufficiency of such consideration should be supported by an appraisal.

- If there are currently outstanding claims against the debtor, any transfer of asset will be suspect. However, if the claims are frivolous or have no substance, they can probably be ignored.
- The debtor transferring the assets should avoid retaining any strings (control) over the assets, and should not retain any benefits from such assets.
- Finally, debtors who have a criminal past will be scrutinized more closely.

The most important badge of fraud is the debtor's financial condition at the time of the transfer, more specifically, if the debtor was insolvent at the time or as a result of the transfer, that is an important indication of actual intent. The insolvency situation is discussed in more detail below.

iii. Overcoming the Badges

Once the creditor produces enough badges to establish actual intent, the debtor will need to make a showing that while the badges of fraud were present, for some reason the transfer was not fraudulent.

Reliance on the advice of counsel is a common way to mitigate the badges. If the debtor seeks the advice or opinion of an attorney prior to the transfer, and is advised that the proposed transfer will not constitute a fraudulent conveyance, that strongly supports the debtor's position. Remember, the debtor is trying to establish lack of intent to defraud, and seeking legal advice is a good way of accomplishing that.

However, reliance on advice of counsel is not an absolute shield. The debtor will have to establish that his or her reliance was reasonable, that all of the relevant facts were disclosed to the attorney and that the counsel's interpretation of the law was also reasonable.[71] Even if reliance is established, it is not a *per se* absolute defense, but only one of the factors that the court may consider.

The more frequent method of overcoming the badges of fraud is by establishing an independent business purpose for the transfer. For example, a transfer of life insurance into an irrevocable trust for the benefit of one's children certainly triggers some badges of fraud. But keeping in mind that the badges are used solely to infer intent, they can be overcome by establishing that the trust was set up as an estate planning tool, to minimize the debtor's estate on death. A transfer of assets to an entity controlled by the debtor may also trigger certain badges, but the debtor may attempt to establish that he was planning on engaging in a joint venture with other investors by utilizing the entity.

In asset protection planning, as in tax planning, establishing a viable independent business purpose is crucial. To be more effective, the business purpose should be established (*i.e.*, papered and documented) prior to the transfer.

b. Any Creditor

The actual intent test looks to the debtor's intent to defraud "any" creditor. The modifier "any" is very important. A creditor seeking to set aside a conveyance as a fraudulent transfer need not show that the debtor intended to defraud

---

[71] See, e.g., In re Bateman, 646 F. 2d 1220 (8th Cir. 1981).

this specific creditor. The creditor need only show that at the time of the transfer the debtor sought to defraud some specific creditor.

However, while the debtor need only to have intent to defraud "any" creditor, that statement is somewhat misleading. For fraudulent transfer purposes, the world of creditors is divided into three classes: present creditors, future creditors, and future potential creditors.

CCC Section 3439.04 provides that the transfer may be deemed fraudulent "whether the creditor's claim arises before or after the transfer was made." This would seem to imply that any creditor, present or future, would be protected by the UFTA; which conflicts with the common law concept of the free alienability of property by its owner.

While the UFTA clearly applies to present creditors,[72] the distinction between a future creditor and a future potential creditor is not as clear. A future creditor is defined as a creditor whose claim arises after the transfer in question, but there was a foreseeable connection between the creditor and the debtor at the time of the transfer.[73] A future potential or contingent creditor is one whose claim arises after the transfer, but there was no foreseeable connection be-

---

[72] A present creditor is a creditor holding a matured claim. Thus, creditors who filed a lawsuit, received a judgment or were just run over by the debtor (and thus accrued a claim against the debtor) are present creditors.

[73] For example, a doctor's pool of patients are future creditors of the doctor, as there is a foreseeable connection. (However, what is a foreseeable connection for an ob-gyn may not be a foreseeable connection for an oncologist.) The homeowner is the future creditor of the building contractor, because there is a foreseeable connection.

tween the creditor and the debtor at the time of the transfer.[74]

Generally, a future creditor is one who holds a contingent, unliquidated or unmatured claim against the debtor. A transfer is fraudulent as to a future creditor if there is fraudulent intent directed at the creditor at the time of the transfer. For example, if a debtor is about to default on a personal guarantee, and transfers her assets in anticipation of such default, the holder of the guarantee is a future creditor and the transfer is made with intent to defraud the creditor.

A future creditor must not only be foreseeable at the time of the transfer of assets, the timing of such creditor's claim must be proximate to the time of the transfer. In one case, the court defined the term "future creditor" as on whose claim is "reasonably foreseen as arising in the immediate future."[75]

Future potential creditors are distinguished from future creditors by the fact that there is no intent to defraud a particular future potential creditor. For example, a debtor is worried that he has insufficient automobile insurance coverage and transfers his assets. Those who may in the future be run over by the debtor are future potential creditors, as there is no intent to run over a specific person.

Because the UFTA is commonly held to apply only to future creditors, but not to future potential creditors, asset protection planning focuses on future potential creditors.

---

[74] For example, someone the debtor may run over tomorrow, is a future potential creditor today.
[75] Leopold v. Tuttle, 549 A. 2d 151, 154 (Penn. 1988).

To summarize, only a present or future creditor may bring a fraudulent transfer action under the actual intent test. Future potential creditors do not have standing to bring a fraudulent transfer action. It is also impossible for the debtor to have actual intent to defraud a person of whose existence the debtor is not aware.

Thus, the word "any" is somewhat misleading, because it does not really mean "any." The debtor must have a specific creditor in mind to form actual intent.

This distinction between what types of creditors are protected under the UFTA is easier to grasp by trying to visualize the faces of one's creditors. As a rule of thumb, if the debtor knows what the creditor looks like at the time of the transfer, that creditor is protected.

For example, if the lawsuit has been filed prior to the transfer of assets, the debtor knows what that creditor/plaintiff looks like. Thus, present creditors can be visualized with great specificity. If at the time of the transfer of assets the debtor has a good idea of what the creditor looks like (an accountant's pool of clients, a doctor's pool of patients, the business owner's creditor) these are future creditors. If the debtor cannot picture what the creditor looks like because the debtor is not even aware of the existence of this creditor, this is a future potential creditor.

Of course, this is only a rule of thumb, but it does make these concepts easier to understand. The focus is on the relationship between the debtor and the creditor at the time of the transfer, as demonstrated in these examples:

Example 1: Dr. Brown runs over an old lady and her poodle. Fearing an imminent lawsuit, Dr. Brown transfers $20 to his brother. At the moment the old lady was run over, she became a present creditor.[76] Dr. Brown had specific intent to defraud her, and the old lady can seek to set aside the transfer of $20.

Example 2: Dr. Brown transfers $20 to his brother. Three days later he runs over the old lady and the unfortunate poodle. In this case, there is no foreseeable connection between Dr. Brown and the old lady at the time of the transfer of money. The old lady has no standing to attempt to set aside the transfer of money.

Example 3: Dr. Brown signed a contract to purchase a stethoscope. The other party to the contract became a "present creditor" as soon as Dr. Brown signed the contract.

Example 4: Dr. Brown is experiencing early stages of epilepsy. Afraid of mucking up a surgery, he transfers $20 to his brother. Two months later, Dr. Brown has an epilepsy attack during a surgery, and mayhem ensues. Can the mutilated patient attempt to set aside the transfer of $20? Because there is a foreseeable connection between the good doctor and the patient at the time of the transfer, and there is some proximity as to the timing of the claim and the transfer, the patient is a future creditor and has standing to challenge the transfer. Of course, an argument can be made in Dr. Brown's favor if the doctor-patient relationship did

---

[76] The old lady is a present creditor because she has a claim against Dr. Brown. A claim is a "right to payment, whether or not the right is reduced to judgment, liquidated, unliquidated, fixed, contingent, matured, unmatured, disputed, undisputed, legal, equitable, secured or unsecured." UFTA Section 1(3).

not exist at the time of the transfer. There is no clear guidance on this point.

c. Constructive Intent

CCC Sections 3439.04(b)(1), 3439.04(b)(2) and 3439.05 also provide that a transfer may be fraudulent without any actual intent to defraud a creditor if a transfer was made without receiving an equivalent value in return,[77] in one of three situations:

1. When a debtor was engaged or was about to engage in a business or a transaction for which the remaining assets of the debtor were unreasonably small in relation to the business or transaction;
2. The debtor intended to incur, or believed or reasonably should have believed that he or she would incur debts beyond his or her ability to pay as they became due; and
3. The debtor was insolvent at the time of the transfer, or the debtor became insolvent as a result of the transfer.

The fair market value of the property received in return is an important element of the fraudulent transfer laws. As a matter of fact, a creditor would have a most difficult time

---

[77] The law generally does not require the debtor to receive an exact same fair market value in return, but the values must be reasonably proximate. Practitioners generally use 70% as a guideline amount.

proving a fraudulent transfer where the debtor received full fair market value in return.

Fair market value is established through appraisals and valuations. It is very important to document the sufficiency of the value at the time of the transfer. Likewise, it is important to document that both the valuation and the transfer were achieved at arm's length. When a debtor transfers assets for adequate consideration, even if the transfer is to a family member, establishing the fraud element is exceedingly difficult.

Often, financially distressed debtors are forced to sell their assets, such as in a foreclosure sale or other bargain sales. In such circumstances, assets are frequently sold for less than the hypothetical fair market value. The Supreme Court held that in such circumstances, the consideration received in a forced sale constitutes equivalent value.[78] However, the protection of this Supreme Court ruling applies only when there is an opportunity for competitive bidding. For example, the consideration received in a foreclosure sale will be deemed sufficient only if the sale was open to public bidding.

The use of partnerships becomes of great importance in reducing the amount of acceptable fair market value. Because partnership interests can frequently be discounted for lack of control and lack of marketability, the debtor may be able to sell a partnership interest at a discount and still satisfy the adequate fair market value test. However, to comply with the above referenced Supreme Court ruling, it may be advisable to disclose the sale in a local newspaper, thus,

---

[78] In re BFP, 511 U. S. 531, 545 (1994).

theoretically, opening the sale of the interest to public bidding.

Under the actual intent test discussed above, both present and future creditors can bring an action to void a transfer. That is not the case under the constructive fraud test. Under this test, only present creditors can challenge the transfer. Future creditors must always establish actual intent, which is generally a lot more difficult than showing that the debtor was insolvent and made a transfer for less than full consideration.

The insolvency situation is the most important one, as it is most frequently applied, and we will start there.

i. Insolvency

The debtor's financial condition, specifically the question of whether the debtor is insolvent, is by far the most important inquiry under the actual intent or the constructive fraud tests. In any asset protection case, this should always be the initial query. It is often recommended that the client's accountant prepare a current balance sheet, on a fair market value (not book) basis. While solvency does not mean that the debtor is in the clear to make any transfer, insolvency usually leads directly to a fraudulent transfer finding.

Constructing the debtor's balance sheet is not a straight forward exercise in accounting. The assets must be reflected on the balance at their fair market values, and both assets and liabilities while determined on the date of the transfer, must take certain other factors into account.

Thus, for example, in determining the debtor's assets, anticipated income streams, foreseeable capital sources, and loans must be taken into account. This means that a business must be valued as a going concern, accounting for future anticipated cash flows. Value is usually determined by assuming that the debtor would have a reasonable amount of time to sell his or her assets. Consequently, no liquidation discounts are applied. This is obviously favorable to the debtor who wants to establish his or her solvency.

Because valuations frequent rely on expert testimony, the value of a contemporaneous appraisal cannot be overstressed.

Certain types of assets cannot be taken into account (obviously to the detriment of the debtor trying to establish his or her solvency):

- Exempt assets—such as assets protected by the available state or bankruptcy exemptions (like the homestead exemption), and other unreachable assets, such as when the debtor is a beneficiary of a discretionary or spendthrift trust.
- Assets that are transferred to defraud, hinder or delay a creditor.
- Assets that are outside of the jurisdiction of the court—such as assets located in foreign jurisdictions.
- Assets that have been transferred to entities (partnerships, limited liability companies) must be valued by applying valuation discounts.

Under the UFCA (the predecessor statutes to our current fraudulent transfer laws) liabilities were taken into account on their face value and even frivolous lawsuits served to reduce the debtor's solvency. Under the UFTA and the bankruptcy code, liabilities must be discounted from their face value to reflect the probability that they will mature and accrue. This means that a $10 million lawsuit filed against the debtor, where the debtor has an 80% chance of prevailing, must be reflected on the debtor's balance sheet as a $2 million liability.

While certain contingent liabilities must be accounted for, future liabilities are not taken into account. Thus, as a general rule, liabilities that only have to be footnoted for GAAP are not taken into account, because they are future liabilities.

As a rule of thumb, assets are usually valued from the standpoint of the creditor—what would the creditor realize from these assets. Liabilities are valued from the standpoint of the debtor—what is the debtor expected to pay.

Only present creditors may pursue an action for constructive fraud under the insolvency test. No future or future potential creditor has standing. However, it should be kept in mind that insolvency, with respect to a future creditor, may still be used as a badge of fraud.

ii. Overcoming Insolvency

While not immediately apparent from the language of the California Civil Code, it is not enough for a creditor to show that an insolvent debtor made a transfer for less than full and adequate consideration. There must be some connection between the insolvency and the transfer. Usually, this means that there must be more to these two elements (transfer and insolvency) than their proximity in time.

For example, in Credit Managers Association of South. Cal. v. Federal Co., 629 F. Supp. 175, 184 (1985), a transfer by the debtor for less than full consideration followed shortly by a loss of a big customer and a labor strike that made the debtor insolvent was not fraudulent. The court focused on the fact that the imminent insolvency was not anticipated at the time of the transfer. Thus, an unforeseen event that makes the debtor insolvent may be sufficient to rebut the constructive fraud test.

iii. Businesses with Unreasonably Small Assets

Insolvency is one of three circumstances when a transfer of assets for less than adequate consideration will constitute constructive fraud. Another set of circumstances giving rise to constructive fraud is when the debtor makes a transfer and retains a small amount of assets, and it is foreseeable that such small amount of assets will be insufficient to meet the obligations of the debtor.

This test focuses on companies and not individuals (technically, it may apply to individuals as well, but is rarely applied in practice), and only on those companies that require capital to operate (*i.e.*, holding companies are not subject to this test).

This test will protect those creditors who engage in a business transaction with a debtor company that does not retain sufficient assets to pay its liabilities. However, not all transfers will be suspect under this test. This test, unlike the insolvency test, does not focus on the debtor's balance sheet on a particular date, but looks forward beyond the date of the transfer. The test focuses on the debtor's continued ability to operate its business, which means that those transfers that do not diminish that ability, cannot be voided by a creditor.

For example, if a business engages in a sale and lease-back transaction which reduces its operating costs, that will not be treated as a transfer challengeable under constructive fraud.

Whether or not the business is too thinly capitalized to pay its liabilities as they come due is a question of fact with respect to each specific business. Factors that must be taken into account include the volatility of this particular business (greater volatility requires greater capitalization) and future expansion plans.

As with the insolvency factor, it is important to demonstrate the client's continued business vitality following a transfer by enlisting the help of client's accountants and financial advisors.

iv. Incurring Debt beyond Ability to Pay

The third set of circumstances that may trigger constructive fraud on a transfer for less than full and adequate consideration is for debts incurred beyond the debtor's ability to pay.

This test is very similar to the above test, except that it focuses mainly on transfers made by individuals, and not businesses. In practice, the two tests are rarely distinguished, as both focus on a debtor's continued ability to pay its obligations.

The only distinction between the two tests is that the first one, because it relates to companies, focuses on business debts, while the second one focuses on personal obligations.

4. The "Good Faith" Defense

CCC Section 3439.08 provides that a transfer or an obligation is not voidable under Section 3439.04(a) against a person who took in good faith and for a reasonably equivalent value or against any subsequent transferee or obligee. This means that even if the debtor acted in bad faith and intended to commit actual fraud, the creditor or the bankruptcy trustee will not be able to void the transfer to a person who purchased in "good faith."

In order for a purchaser to be protected from the application of the UFTA under the good faith exemption, the purchaser must **(i)** take the property in good faith; **(ii)** take the property without knowledge of fraud on the creditor; and **(iii)** provide fair consideration in exchange for the property received. Transferees cannot simply rely on what is known or not known to them. They have a duty to investigate, if certain facts put them on notice.

5. Practical Implications of a Fraudulent Transfer

Thoughts of fraudulent transfers induce great fear and trepidation, and they have replaced the boogey man in the closet to scare children into being good. Because of their name, fraudulent transfers are often equated with fraud, and would-be transferees visualize dark prison cells and hefty monetary penalties.

However, under California law, if a transfer is fraudulent, that usually means that the creditor can set aside the transfer and proceed after the transferee to recover the transferred asset. A patient files a malpractice suit against Dr. Brown. Dr. Brown promptly transfers his golden scalpel to his uncle for safe-keeping. The patient-creditor has no connection to the uncle and cannot sue the uncle to recover the scalpel. However, if the creditor proves that the transfer of the scalpel by Dr. Brown to his uncle was a fraudulent transfer, the creditor can set aside the transfer and get the scalpel from the uncle. (If the creditor successfully establishes that a transfer is fraudulent, then the uncle—the transferee—is deemed as holding the transferred property in trust for the creditor.)

Consequently, if a creditor proves that a transfer is fraudulent, that simply makes the transfer ineffective. If the debtor has no means to protect her assets other than to engage in a transfer that may be fraudulent, what is the downside to the debtor in engaging in such a transfer? In the worst case scenario, the debtor loses her assets, which is exactly the same position she would have been in had she not engaged in the transfer in the first place. But there is a definite upside in engaging in the transfer because there is usually no certainty that a creditor would bring a fraudulent transfer action or that the creditor would then be successful in proving a fraudulent transfer and then manage to actually recover the asset from the transferee.

This practical implication of a fraudulent transfer is rarely discussed in the asset protection literature. Lawyers should never advise clients to engage in a fraudulent transfer, and knowingly engaging in a fraudulent transfer is certainly unethical. However, because this area of the law is so often unclear, when it cannot be determined with any certainty whether a transfer will be deemed fraudulent, and the debtor is left with no other choices, the debtor should consider taking the more aggressive approach to asset protection planning. Again, what is the downside?[79]

Finally, in some cases debtors can engage in a fraudulent transfer without any recourse by the creditor. For example, as discussed below, a transfer into an ERISA qualified retirement plan cannot be set aside by a creditor even if it is fraudulent. Fraudulent transfer laws are state statutes and are always trumped by the application of federal statutes (ERISA), or state constitutions (Florida and Texas homestead exemptions).

The following case study will illustrate the practical consequences of last minute asset protection planning.

C. Case Study on Last Minute Asset Protection Planning

1. Facts

Our case study will explore the unfortunate situation of George and Marilyn, a fictitious couple that very closely resembles so many of our asset protection clients in this

[79] It should be noted that Section 531of the California Penal Code provides that engaging or assisting in a fraudulent transfer is a misdemeanor. In practice, to the knowledge of this author, this section is never enforced, probably because it may be impossible to prove the required "intent" beyond a reasonable doubt.

economic downturn. George and Marilyn are in their late sixties, retired, live in California, and have the following assets: a personal residence worth $500,000 with no mortgage; a tenancy in common interest in an apartment building worth $250,000; an office building with no equity (located in Texas); $150,000 in a bank account; $300,000 in a brokerage account; and $150,000 in George's IRA.

Until recently, George and Marilyn owned several apartment buildings. Those were sold in 2008, generating $3 million of sale proceeds. The sale proceeds were used to buy the office building in Texas for $7 million, with $4 million financed and personally guaranteed by George. Several months following the purchase of the office building, the building's only tenant filed for bankruptcy. George and Marilyn carried the building for a year, trying to find a new tenant, with no success. They feel that they cannot sustain carrying the building for much longer and plan on defaulting in three months. The building is now worth $1.5 million.

We will examine whether fraudulent transfer laws prevent George and Marilyn from pursuing asset protection, and, if not, what structures are available to protect each asset, the substantive law behind each structure and their practical implications.

2. Of Ivory Towers and Fraudulent Transfers

There is only one chink in the armor of any asset protection structure—the creditor's ability to challenge the structure as a fraudulent transfer. There are no other legal grounds that would allow the lender to reach the assets that

George and Marilyn would transfer into one of the structures discussed below. If George and Marilyn can escape or survive a fraudulent transfer attack, then any structure used to protect assets works. The choices presented by the structures described below will make fraudulent transfers more or less difficult to prove, or if a fraudulent transfer is proven, will make the assets more or less desirable to pursue.

Not all asset transfers are subject to a fraudulent transfer challenge. For a transfer to be deemed a "fraudulent transfer" the creditor has to either demonstrate specific intent on the debtor's part to "hinder, delay or defraud" a specific creditor's collection efforts (the "actual intent" test), or establish that the transfer is constructively fraudulent.[80] A transfer is constructively fraudulent if it is **(1)** for less than fair market value and **(2)** the debtor is insolvent at the time or as a result of the transfer.[81]

Much has been written on the subject of fraudulent transfers and we will not revisit it here.[82] Instead, the following are a few important legal and practical elements and consequences that are of interest to George and Marilyn.

Under the actual intent test, the lender would have to demonstrate George and Marilyn's intent underlying the transfer of assets. Intent is demonstrated by examining the circumstantial evidence surrounding the transfer, the so-

---

[80] Uniform Fraudulent Transfer Act ("UFTA") §§ 4(a) and 5(a). The UFTA has been codified by each state. The Bankruptcy Code § 548 contains its own version of the UFTA. The UFTA and Bankruptcy Code § 548 are so similar, that either may be used in litigation. *Donell v. Kowell*, 533 F.3d 762, 770 (9th Cir. 2008).
[81] UFTA § 5(a).
[82] See, for example, Stein, Jacob, Asset Protection May Risk Fraudulent Transfer Violations, Estate Planning, August 2010.

called "badges of fraud." Establishing intent is always a subjective analysis by the court. Other than the arguments and the spin of the parties, there are few objective factors to consider. For that reason, in practice, creditors prefer to focus on establishing constructive fraud, a determination that is purely objective.

While establishing constructive fraud is straightforward, only "present creditors" may use the constructive fraud test.[83] It may be argued that the lender holding George's personal guaranty is not a present creditor until after George defaults on the note (there is no breach of contract until default). If that is the case, avoiding a fraudulent transfer attack is greatly simplified—transfer assets in exchange for fair market value or do not engage in a transfer that results in insolvency. More on that below.

There is rarely certainty in asset protection planning. Any transfer of assets may be challenged by a creditor as a fraudulent transfer and possibly challenged successfully. How does that hinder the actions that our hypothetical clients will take to protect their assets?

George and Marilyn's decision tree is simple. They can choose to do nothing to protect their assets, either because they are worried about a fraudulent transfer challenge or for any other reason, or they can choose to implement an asset protection plan. Doing nothing is easy to implement and inexpensive, at first, but will result in a close to 100 percent chance of them losing all their assets in the event of a

---

[83] A present creditor is a creditor whose claim arose before the transfer was made. UFTA § 5(a). Contrast that with a future creditor, a creditor whose claim arises before the transfer is made. UFTA § 4(a).

judgment. As Wayne Gretzky used to say, "One hundred percent of the shots you *do not* take, do not go in."

If George and Marilyn choose to protect their assets, the lender may challenge the transfers as fraudulent transfers; it will then either prevail or lose that challenge. Even if the lender prevails, it may still be unable to recover the transferred assets.

The creditor's sole practical remedy in the event of a successful fraudulent transfer challenge is to unwind the transfer (*i.e.*, reach the transferred assets).[84] The debtor is not subject to damages, criminal penalties or caning. The exercise of this remedy will place George and Marilyn in exactly the same position had they chosen to do nothing. Consequently, our clients can only improve their position by trying to protect their assets. In their case, the risk of a fraudulent transfer challenge carries no downside. Even the transaction costs incurred in implementing the asset protection structure are not a consideration, as that money would have been lost to the lender in any case.

The analysis of a fraudulent transfer challenge is therefore an analysis of legal theory as it applies to fraudulent transfers and an analysis of the practical consequences of ignoring such theory. Most attorneys rely purely on theory in making their predictions as to the efficacy of an asset protection plan. If theory leads to prediction, then theory coupled with practical experience leads to an accurate prediction.

A further practical planning point to consider is the available case law. If one peruses the available court deci-

---

[84] UFTA § 7(a)(1).

sions on fraudulent transfers, there are a great many that hold in favor of a creditor, leading the observer to conclude that most fraudulent transfer challenges are successful. In practice, that is not so. Proving a fraudulent transfer, especially under the actual intent test, is not an easy task. The decided cases present a selection bias. It is always the creditor's choice to litigate a possible fraudulent transfer, and weak cases are less likely to be litigated. A great majority of cases are settled without litigation or settled during litigation, and the existence of an asset protection structure, whether or not it is susceptible to a fraudulent transfer attack, will almost always result in a better settlement for the debtor.

Any transfer susceptible to a fraudulent transfer attack implicates ethical considerations. This author certainly does not advocate that an attorney should behave unethically. However, this author does believe that the ultimate arbiter of what is right and what is wrong is the client. The client should decide whether an asset protection structure should be implemented. The lawyer's job is to educate and advise, not to make a decision that will so greatly impact the client's life. As an aside, we have learned in our practice that what many deem ethical or unethical will vary greatly depending on whether it is their own assets that are at stake, or a stranger's.

Planning early is always the best defense against a fraudulent transfer challenge. The debtor will either lack the requisite intent or will not have a present creditor. When planning late, allow your client to consider the practical consequences of his choices, and not just legal theory.

3. Planning Options

a. Marilyn Comes to the Rescue

While asset protection planning is generally asset specific, there is one planning option that will span all assets. Because George signed the personal guaranty and Marilyn did not, the lender cannot sue Marilyn. Once the lender obtains a judgment against George, the lender may pursue collection actions against his assets only.[85]

In a community property state, all assets that are community property may be pursued by a creditor of either spouse.[86] This means that even though the lender may not sue Marilyn, all of the assets owned by George and Marilyn as community property are subject to the lender's collection remedies.

In most[87] community property states, a frequently utilized asset protection technique is a transmutation agreement.[88] This is a form of a post-nuptial agreement that is used to convert community property to separate property or vice versa. A typical transmutation agreement will state that the spouses are terminating their community property interests in all or some of their assets and are creating separate property interests in such assets.

This would mean that George and Marilyn can agree that some of their assets will become the separate property

---

[85] Cal. Code Civ. Proc. § 695.010(a).
[86] Cal. Fam. Code § 910(a).
[87] Nevada, for example, makes transmutations ineffective as to third parties. Nev. Rev. Stat. § 123.220(1).
[88] Cal. Fam. Code § 850.

of Marilyn and therefore would not be owned by George. Assets not owned by George are not reachable by his creditors.[89]

Transmutation agreements enjoyed recent notoriety during the divorce proceeding of Frank and Jamie McCourt, the owners of the Los Angeles Dodgers. The McCourts entered into a transmutation agreement to protect their real estate from the creditors of the Dodgers. Frank signed a personal guaranty to the lenders; Jamie did not. In their transmutation agreement, the McCourts made the Dodgers Frank's separate property and the real estate Jamie's separate property. If the baseball franchise could not satisfy its financial obligations, Frank's creditors could look only to his assets to satisfy the personal guaranty. Jamie's assets would be off limits.

As the McCourts had discovered, a transmutation agreement is a binding legal document for all purposes, including a divorce. That means that George and Marilyn must be advised of that risk and it also means that the possibility of a divorce is a reason to allocate the assets to the two spouses equally, based on fair market value. This way, if one of them files for divorce, there is no downside—community property would have been split equally in a divorce.

Another reason to split the assets equally is to minimize the risk of a successful fraudulent transfer attack. If the assets are split evenly, then George and Marilyn would transfer assets to each other for fair market value.

---

[89] Cal. Code Civ. Proc. § 695.010(a).

There are usually several ways to split assets between the two spouses. Each spouse can be given a one-half interest in each asset, resulting in a mathematically precise split, or specific assets can be allocated to each spouse.

If possible,[90] the latter approach is preferable. Analyzing the assets that George and Marilyn own, we will discover that real estate is more difficult to protect than other assets, that bank and brokerage accounts are more desirable for a creditor to pursue, and the clients have a great deal of affinity for their personal residence.

The preferred allocation of assets would then be to transfer those assets that are more difficult to protect to Marilyn, even if it means moving liquid assets to George. In our case study assets allocated to Marilyn would include the personal residence, the tenancy in common interest in the apartment building and the office building. George would receive the remaining assets, which include the bank account, the brokerage account and the IRA.

The allocations, by value, are not exactly equal. Marilyn would receive $750,000 worth of assets and George $600,000. There are three ways to deal with this discrepancy: revalue the assets (real estate valuations are often subjective), give George a small tenancy in common interest in real estate, or create an additional benefit for George or a detriment for Marilyn. An example of the third option would be a full or partial waiver of spousal support by Marilyn in the event of a divorce. Such a waiver could be val-

---

[90] Would not be possible if the spouses owned one asset, or several assets with greatly divergent values, making it mathematically impossible to achieve an equal split overall.

ued and easily be made equal to the extra $150,000 Marilyn is receiving in the transmutation.

The following is some wisdom from the trenches: **(i)** the split of the assets does not have to be mathematically precise, just close to it; **(ii)** for the transmutation of the real estate to be effective as to third parties, the transmutation, or a memorandum of the transmutation, must be recorded; **(iii)** the parties do not have to be represented by separate counsel (lack of separate counsel is relevant only for divorce purposes, not for debtor creditor purposes); **(iv)** on the first death, the spouses will lose the step up in basis for the assets owned by the surviving spouse; **(v)** not all assets owned by the spouses need to be covered by the transmutation agreement; and **(vi)** it is possible to transmute assets to separate property but leave wages as community property.

Similar planning is possible but difficult in common law states. For example, if George and Marilyn were living in New York, they would have no community property. George would have his separate property and Marilyn hers.[91] For George to be able to transfer assets to Marilyn in exchange for fair market value, Marilyn would have to transfer some of her assets back to George. This technique may still be useful if George owns difficult to protect assets and Marilyn owns easy to protect assets.

In many states spouses should also consider taking title to property as tenants by the entirety. This is a form of a concurrent estate in real property where each spouse owns an undivided whole of the property. Most states that allow

---

[91] The concept of marital property is irrelevant for debtor-creditor purposes.

spouses to hold title to property as tenants by the entirety do not allow a creditor of one spouse to place a lien on the property, as that would interfere with the rights of the other spouse in such property.[92] Some of the states that protect tenancy by the entirety interests allow the debtor-spouse's interest to be reached on the death of the non-debtor spouse.[93]

b. Real Estate

George and Marilyn have three basic options to protect the equity in their real estate:[94] they can sell, encumber or transfer title.

An outright sale of the real estate affords the most protection. Real estate is not a fungible asset and can never be protected in a "bulletproof" manner. Once the real estate is converted into a liquid asset, it may be possible to protect such liquid asset with great efficacy. The outright sale of the real estate is a radical approach. George and Marilyn will have to pack up their belongings, find a new place to live and incur capital gains on the sale. However, even with that in mind, the outright sale may be a better option than

---

[92] See, e.g., *Citizens' Saving Bank v. Astrin*, 44 Del. 451, 61 A. 2d 419 (1948), *Amadon v. Amadon*, 359 Pa. 434, 59 A. 2d 135 (1948); *Keen v. Keen*, 191 Md. 31, 60 A.2d 200 (1948).

[93] *Sloan v. Sloan*, 182 Tenn. 162, 184 S.W.2d 391 (1945).

[94] With real estate, it is always equity, and not the real estate itself, that is being protected. A creditor's remedy with respect to debtor's real estate is limited to placing a judgment lien on the real estate and then foreclosing on such lien. See, e.g., Cal. Code of Civ. Proc. §§ 697.310(a), 701.510 and 701.810.

allowing the creditor to record a lien on the real estate and then foreclose.

Encumbering the real estate involves using the real estate as collateral to secure a loan. It may be used as collateral to secure an existing obligation or a newly created obligation. George and Marilyn should be cautioned that if the newly created obligation is to a family member, it may be scrutinized closely by the creditor and by the court. For the encumbrance to work, it needs to be a real, bona-fide encumbrance and not simply the recording of a deed of trust without any supporting substance.

Transferring title out of the debtor's name is the most frequently used approach. We have already examined this approach in the context of having George transfer title to the real estate to Marilyn. Other possibilities may include transferring title to a limited liability company or limited partnership or to an irrevocable trust.

c. LLCs and Limited Partnerships

Unlike most assets, a membership interest in a limited liability company or a partnership interest in a limited or general partnership is not subject to attachment by a creditor.[95] The creditor's remedy with respect to these assets is

---

[95] §§ 503 of the Unif. Ltd. Liab. Co. Act (2006) ("ULLCA"), Rev. Unif. Part. Act (1994) ("RUPA") and Unif. Lim. Part. Act (2001) ("ULPA"). All states have enacted the uniform acts in some way. See, e.g., Alaska Stat., § 32.06.504, Del. Code Ann. 6, § 18-703, Cal. Corp. Code § 17302, Nev. Rev. Stat. § 86.401.

limited to a charging order and/or a foreclosure of the assignable interest.[96]

The charging order is a lien on the debtor's transferable interest in the entity.[97] A "transferable interest" is defined in the uniform acts as a right to receive distributions.[98]

An interest in an LLC or a limited/general partnership commonly consists of two bundles of rights: **(1)** an economic interest (also called assignable, transferable or distributional)—the right to receive distributions of cash and property and the corresponding allocations of income, gain, loss and deduction, and **(2)** management and voting rights.[99] All available creditor remedies (charging order and/or foreclosure) are directed solely at the economic interest; management and voting rights are untouchable. The uniform acts go as far as to provide that: "While in effect, that [charging] order entitles the judgment creditor to whatever distributions would otherwise be due to the partner or transferee whose interest is subject to the order. The creditor has no say in the timing or amount of those distributions. The charging order does not entitle the creditor to accelerate any distributions or to otherwise interfere with the management and activities of the limited partnership."[100]

The creditor's inability to vote the charged interest or participate in the management of the entity is at the heart of

---

[96] *Id.*
[97] ULLCA, RUPA, ULPA § 504. Notice that ULLCA uses the term "distributional" and state law often uses the term "assignable."
[98] See, e.g., ULLCA § 101(6), ULPA § 102(22).
[99] ULLCA § 101(5), Comments; Cal. Corp. Code § 17001(n).
[100] ULPA § 703, Comments.

the asset protection efficacy of the charging order. If the partnership or the LLC halts all distributions, the creditor has no ability to force the distributions. Because the charging order liens only those distributions made to the member in his capacity as a member, debtors can frequently pull assets out of the entity solution using loans and guaranteed payments.[101]

The foreclosure remedy is rarely useful to a creditor. The uniform acts and the corresponding state acts clearly provide that only the charged interest (*i.e.*, the economic/ assignable/ transferable/ distributional interest) may be foreclosed upon, and further provide that the purchaser at the foreclosure sale has only the rights of a transferee.[102] To grant the purchaser of the foreclosed interest an interest greater than the right to receive distributions would mean granting to the purchaser voting and management rights associated with the debtor's interest in the entity. That would be contrary to the very reason why charging order statutes exist in the first place.[103]

The exclusivity of the charging order appears to be expressly set forth only in the Delaware LLC statute (it is also

---

[101] ULLCA § 101(5).

[102] ULLCA § 503(c), "... the court may foreclose the lien and order the sale of the transferable interest. The purchaser at the foreclosure sale only obtains the transferable interest, does not thereby become a member..."

[103] For a great state-by-state analysis of charging order statutes and the foreclosure remedy, see Bishop, "Fifty State Series: LLC Charging Order Statutes" table, that may be accessed at http://ssrn.com/abstract=1542244.

present in several other countries).[104] Other state statutes either expressly authorize the foreclosure remedy and provide that the charging order and the foreclosure are the exclusive remedies,[105] or do not address the foreclosure remedy but speak to exclusivity,[106] or do not address the foreclosure remedy or the exclusivity.[107]

In a recent Florida Supreme Court decision, the exclusivity of the charging order was denied to a single-member LLC and the levy of the LLC interest was allowed.[108] The Florida Supreme Court reasoned that: **(i)** under the Florida statute the assignee becomes a member unless the non-debtor members fail to consent (and in a single-member LLC there are no other members who can fail to consent), and **(ii)** the comparable Florida limited partnership act does make the charging order remedy the exclusive remedy. Practitioners establishing LLCs in states lacking the exclusivity language in their charging order statutes should be mindful of the Olmstead ruling and seek to establish multi-member LLCs.

---

[104] Del. Code Ann. 6, § 18-703(d). " The entry of a charging order is the exclusive remedy by which a
judgment creditor of a member or of a member's assignee may satisfy a judgment out of the judgment debtor's limited liability company interest." [Emphasis added.] St. Vincent and the Grenadines LLC Act (2008) §61(3).

[105] See, e.g., Cal. Corp. Code § 17302(b)

[106] See, e.g., Nev. Rev. Stat. § 86.401(2). " This section: (a) Provides the exclusive remedy by which a judgment creditor of a member or an assignee of a member may satisfy a judgment out of the member's interest of the judgment debtor." [Emphasis added.]

[107] See, e.g., Fla. Stat. Ann. § 608.433, Ind. Code Ann. § 23-18-6-7.

[108] *Olmstead v. Federal Trade Commission*, 44 So. 3d 76 (Fla. 2010).

Through the use of artfully crafted entity agreements, practitioners can often greatly improve on the efficacy of the LLC/LP charging order protection. The following are a few pointers to consider.

Only an assignable interest in the entity may be charged by a creditor and the lien attaches only to the assignable interest.[109] The assignability of an interest is governed by the agreement of the members/partners.[110] Consequently, entity agreements drafted with asset protection in mind should either make membership interests (or just economic interests) non-assignable, or make the assignment subject to the prior approval of the manager or a majority of the members. In a single member limited liability company, it is preferable to ban all assignments.

Consider including a poison pill provision in the entity agreement. The poison pill provision will set a predetermined redemption price for a member's interest and is triggered by a collection action against any member. It will help in contentious litigation cases and will prevent a foreclosure sale of the interest.[111]

Take a close look at the distribution clause of the agreement. Most distribution clauses will empower the manager to determine the timing and the amount of the distribution, but when the distribution is made, the manager will have to distribute *pari passu*. A distribution will be *pari passu* only if made to all the members/partners in accordance with their percentage interests, or to none. In the

---

[109] See, e.g., Cal. Corp. Code §§ 17302(a) and (b).

[110] See, e.g., Cal. Corp. Code § 17301(a).

[111] Most state statutes allow redemption of the charged interest prior to foreclosure. See, e.g., Cal. Corp. Code § 17302(a).

event of a charging order it may be desirable to withhold distributions solely from the debtor-member, but continue distributing to the other members. A clause should be inserted into the agreement trumping the *pari passu* language in those circumstances.

If George and Marilyn seek to transfer their personal residence to the LLC, they should make certain that for federal income tax purposes the LLC is treated as a disregarded entity. This will allow them to preserve the IRC § 121 gain exclusion. They should also be advised that the homestead exemption will be lost once ownership is transferred to the LLC, and for real estate that is encumbered by debt, the transfer may trigger the "due on sale" clause of the loan agreement.

George and Marilyn can easily transfer their real estate to a limited liability company, exchanging unprotected real estate for a membership interest enjoying the limitations of the charging order protection. As with all other transfers, fraudulent transfer consequences must be carefully examined.

d. Trusts

The conceptual goal of all asset protection planning is two-fold: **(1)** remove the debtor's name from the legal title to his assets, but **(2)** in such a way so that he could retain some beneficial enjoyment and a degree of control. These two goals are incompatible, but may be reconciled with the use of a trust, which will split the legal ownership of the assets from their beneficial enjoyment.[112]

A creditor's ability to satisfy a judgment against a beneficiary's interest in a trust is limited to the beneficiary's interest in such trust.[113] Consequently, the common goal of an asset protection trust is to limit the interests of a beneficiary in such a way so as to preclude creditors from collecting against trust assets.

Every asset protection trust must: **(1)** be irrevocable,[114] **(2)** include a spendthrift clause (a clause precluding a beneficiary from demanding or anticipating distributions, and/or transferring his interest to a third party),[115] **(3)** in most states be for the benefit of someone other than the settlor,[116] and **(4)** provide the trustee with as much discretion as possible.

In the majority of states, if a trust is for the benefit of the settlor, the trust is deemed self-settled, and the beneficial interest retained by the settlor is not protected by the spendthrift clause.[117] Over the past two decades there has been a growing movement by the English common law jurisdic-

---

[112] For an in depth discussion of this topic, see, Stein, Jacob, Importance of Trusts in Asset Protection, Cal. Trusts and Est. Quart. (Winter 2007).

[113] See, e.g., *Garcia v. Merlo* (1960) 177 Cal.App.2d 434; *Booge v. First Trust & Sav. Bank* (1944) 64 Cal.App.2d 532-536; *Estate of Bennett* (1939) 13 Cal.2d 354.

[114] See, e.g., Cal Prob. Code § 18200, Fl. Stat. § 736.0505(1)(a), Restatement (Third) of Trusts, § 58 (2003).

[115] See, e.g., Fl. Stat. § 736.0501. For an explanation of the spendthrift clause, see, Unif. Trust Code §§ 501 and 502; Witkin, Summary of Cal. Law (9th ed., 1990), Trusts, § 165.

[116] See, e.g., Cal. Prob. Code § 15304(a), Fl. Stat. § 736.0505 (1)(b), Id. Stat. § 15-7-502(4).

[117] *Id.*

tions to modernize trust law, which includes affording creditor protection to self-settled trusts.[118]

A trust is generally governed by the law of the jurisdiction that has been designated in the trust agreement as the trust's governing law.[119] There are two exceptions: **(1)** states will not recognize laws of sister states that violate their own public policy, and **(2)** real property will be governed by the law of the jurisdiction that is the property's situs.[120] Consequently, picking the governing law of another jurisdiction will not always work to improve the protection of trust assets.

It is often beneficial to make an asset protection trust discretionary. A trust is called "discretionary" when the trustee has discretion (as to the timing, amount and the identity of the beneficiary) in making distributions.[121] There must not be any trust provisions that mandate a distribution, but there may be provisions that set standards for distributions.[122] Because the trustee is not required to make any distribution to any specific beneficiary, or may choose when and how much to distribute, a beneficiary of a discretionary trust may have such a tenuous interest in the trust so as not to constitute a property right at all. If the beneficiary has no property right, there is nothing for a creditor to pur-

---

[118] See, e.g., Ala. Stat. § 34.40.110; 12 Del. Code § 3570; Nev. Rev. Stat. § 166.010, et. seq.; Mo. Ann. Stat. § 428.005 *et. seq.*; R.I. Gen. Laws §§ 18-9.2; 31 Okla. Stat. Ann. §§ 13, 16; Nevis Intl. Exempt Trust Ord. (1995) § 6(4), St. Vincent Intl. Trusts Act (1996) § 10(4).
[119] Rest. 2d Conf. of Laws § 273(b); Uniform Trust Law § 107(1).
[120] Rest. 2d Conf. of Laws § 280.
[121] 11 Witkin, *Summary of Cal. Law* (9th ed. 1990) Trusts, § 166, p. 1019.
[122] Unif. Trust Act § 506.

sue.[123] The statutes follow this line of reasoning by providing that a trustee cannot be compelled to pay a beneficiary's creditor if the trustee has discretion in making distributions of income and principal.[124]

George and Marilyn may use an irrevocable, spendthrift trust, preferably with discretionary distributions powers conferred on the trustee, to shield their assets. Because the transfer of their assets into the trust may be challenged as a fraudulent transfer, George and Marilyn should consider using a trust governed by Nevada law. Nevada allows for a two-year statute of limitations to challenge the transfer of assets into an irrevocable, spendthrift trust governed by Nevada law.[125]

The following are a few practice pointers to consider.

If a trust is discretionary and the debtor is the trustee, a court may force the debtor-trustee to exercise his discretion to pull the assets out of the trust. Solve that by appointing a third-party trust protector who would be able to fire the debtor as the trustee of the trust, and/or be able to veto any distribution.

If the debtor does not have any family members who may be appointed as the beneficiaries of the trust (to get around the self-settled trust issue), designate the governing law of the state that affords protection to a self-settled trust, and then create a limited liability company owned by the debtor and designate it as the beneficiary of the trust. An-

---

[123] *Magavern v. U.S.*, 550 F.2d 797 (2nd Cir. 1977).

[124] See, e.g., Cal. Prob. Code § 15303(a), Unif. Trust Action § 504(b), Restatement (Second) of Trusts, § 187, Comment E; *U.S. v. O'Shaughnessy*, 517 N.W. 2d 574, 577 (Minn. 1994).

[125] Nev. Rev. Stat. § 166.170.

other alternative is to make the trust a "purpose trust." A purpose trust has no beneficiaries and is established to accomplish a specific purpose.[126]

Be careful not to include a general power of appointment as that will cause the trust assets to be reachable by the power holder's creditors.[127] Also, be careful in drafting remainder interests or reversions (as in qualified personal residence trusts). These clauses often return trust assets to the settlor's estate, allowing the creditors of the settlor's estate to reach these assets. Consider naming a separate irrevocable trust (inter-vivos or testamentary) as the remainder beneficiary.

For asset protection purposes, it does not matter how a trust is treated for income or gift and estate tax purposes. The trust must simply be irrevocable, spendthrift and discretionary. Consequently, in some cases it may be more advantageous to use trusts that are defective for income tax purposes (grantor trusts under IRC § 671) and/or defective for gift and estate tax purposes (transfer to the trust is an incomplete transfer under IRC §§ 2501 and 2036). Commonly used trust clauses to accomplish the above are the power to substitute assets,[128] the power to lend to the settlor without proper security,[129] and a limited power of appointment retained by the settlor.[130]

---

[126] Id. Stat. § 15-7-601; St. Vincent Intl. Trusts Act (1996) § 12(1).
[127] Restatement (Third) of Trusts, § 74, Comment A (PD) (4-2005).
[128] IRC § 675(4).
[129] IRC § 675(2).
[130] Treas. Reg. § 25.2511-2(a), IRC § 2036(a).

e. LLCs v. Trusts

There are several criteria that help us to determine whether an LLC or an irrevocable trust will be used to hold real estate.

If there is a likelihood of a fraudulent transfer challenge, using an LLC may be preferable as the transfer is not gratuitous; the debtor makes the transfer in exchange for an LLC interest of equivalent value. Avoiding a gratuitous transfer may also be accomplished by selling assets to a trust in exchange for a note (like the intentionally defective grantor trust structure).

If removing assets from the debtor's balance sheet is desirable, only an irrevocable trust will accomplish that. With a trust, the debtor can declare that he owns no assets without perjuring himself.[131] This approach works well with creditors not well versed in collection laws and techniques.

When transferring a personal residence using a trust may avoid the due on sale clause.[132]

f. Liquid Assets

Both LLCs and irrevocable trusts may be used to protect George and Marilyn's liquid assets (bank and brokerage accounts). Because liquid assets by definition are fungible, consider setting up the LLC or the trust offshore.

---

[131] Contrast that with a transfer of assets to an LLC where the debtor changes the asset he owns (*i.e.*, converts real estate into an LLC interest) but still owns some asset.
[132] Garn-St. Germain Depository Institutions Act of 1982 (Pub. L. 97-320).

Recall that with real estate the governing law is the jurisdiction where the real estate is located, but that is not so with personal property.[133] That means that the more favorable—from an asset protection standpoint—laws of a foreign jurisdiction may come into play when protecting liquid assets.

Even if a U.S. judge refuses to recognize the Nevis charging order statute for LLCs, or the St. Vincent and the Grenadines protection for a self-settled irrevocable trust, the creditor's job is made much more difficult and a lot more expensive when assets are placed offshore. When the assets are offshore, in many instances litigation to reach the assets will take place offshore. For any creditor that presents a great risk, forcing the creditor to engage in an economic analysis of the case that is more favorable to the debtor.

The reader should always remember that the goal of asset protection planning is not to set up a structure impervious to creditor claims. Even with an offshore trust holding its assets offshore, the debtor may be directed by the court to return trust assets, and if he fails to do so, hold the debtor in contempt of court.[134] That may happen, but the odds of that happening are very long,[135] and even if it does happen, with the proper structure the debtor will always be able to return the trust assets to the creditor and avoid contempt.

---

[133] Rest. 2d Conf. of Laws § 280.

[134] See, e.g., *F.T.C. v. Affordable Media, LLC*, 179 F.3d 1228 (9th Cir. 1999), *In re Lawrence*, 238 B.R. 498 (Bankr. S.D. Fla. 1999).

[135] See this author's analysis of contempt in the context of foreign trust planning in: Stein, Jacob, Importance of Trusts in Asset Protection, Cal. Trusts and Est. Quart. (Winter 2007).

The contempt consideration is relevant only if there is a better available alternative—some other structure that may afford George and Marilyn better odds of keeping their liquid assets. Even if a structure is not perfect, it may—and likely will—cause the creditor to either abandon its collection efforts or negotiate on terms much more favorable to the debtor.

g. Retirement Plan

There is no better way of protecting assets than with the help of the federal government. The anti-alienation provision of the Employee Retirement Income Security Act of 1974 ("ERISA")[136] absolutely exempts from claims of creditors the assets of pension, profit-sharing, or 401(k) plans.[137] Two exceptions to this absolute protection are carved out for qualified domestic relations orders and claims under the Federal Debt Collection Procedure Act.[138]

Because the protection is set forth in a federal statute, it will trump any state fraudulent transfer law.[139]

Protection of ERISA is afforded to employees only and does not cover employers. The owner of a business is treated as an employer, even though he may also be an employee of the same business, as in a closely-held corporation. Accordingly, ERISA protection does not apply to sole proprietors, to one owner businesses, whether incorporated or

---

[136] 29 U.S.C. §§1001 *et seq.*

[137] *Raymond B. Yates M.D. P.C. Profit Sharing Plan v. Yates*, 124 S. Ct. 1330 (2004).

[138] 29 U.S.C. §1056(d)(3), 28 U.S.C. §3205.

[139] U.S. Const. art. VI, Par. 2.

unincorporated, and to partnerships, unless the plan covers employees other than the owners, partners and their spouses.[140]

Section 541(c)(2) of the Bankruptcy Code provides an exclusion[141] from the debtor's estate of a beneficial interest in a trust that is subject to a restriction that is enforceable under "applicable nonbankruptcy law." The Supreme Court held that "applicable nonbankruptcy law" includes not only traditional spendthrift trusts, but all other laws, including ERISA provisions that require plans to include anti-alienation provisions.[142] Thus, all plans that are required to include anti-alienation provisions pursuant to ERISA are excluded from the debtor's bankruptcy estate.

Perhaps the most telling evidence of ERISA's protection is the Supreme Court's decision in *Guidry v. Sheetmetal Pension Fund.*[143] In *Guidry,* a union official embezzled money from the union and transferred it to his union pension plan. The union official was convicted of the crime of embezzlement and the union attempted to recover the embezzled proceeds from the pension plan. Other than the fact

---

[140] 29 C. F. R. § 2510.3-3(b), 2510.3-3(c); *Giardono v. Jones*, 876 F. 2d 409 (7th Cir. 1989) (sole proprietor denied standing to bring ERISA action); *Pecham v. Board of Trustees, Etc.*, 653 F. 2d 424, 427 (10th Cir. 1981) (sole proprietor is not eligible for protection under ERISA); *In re Witwer*, 148 B. R. 930, 938 (Bankr. C.D. Cal. 1992), aff'd, 163 B. R. 914 (9th Cir. BAP 1993) (debtor's interest in a qualified plan maintained by a corporation of which he was sole shareholder and employee was not protected by ERISA).

[141] An exclusion, as opposed to an exemption, is not limited in amount.

[142] *Patterson v. Shumate*, 112 S. Ct. 2242 (1992).

[143] 493 U. S. 365 (1990).

that the proceeds were embezzled, the transfer to the pension plan was a fraudulent conveyance.

The Court held that the money in the pension plan could not be reached by creditors, whether by way of a constructive trust, writ of garnishment, or otherwise, because of ERISA's anti-alienation requirements.

Unfortunately for George, he does not have an ERISA-qualified[144] retirement plan, he has an IRA. George has three options of protecting his IRA: **(1)** roll it over into a qualified plan, like a 401(k), **(2)** take a distribution, pay the tax and protect the proceeds along with the other liquid assets, or **(3)** rely on the state law exemption for IRAs.

For example, the California exemption statute provides that IRAs and self-employed plans' assets "are exempt only to the extent necessary to provide for the support of the judgment debtor when the judgment debtor retires and for the support of the spouse and dependents of the judgment debtor, taking into account all resources that are likely to be available for the support of the judgment debtor when the judgment debtor retires."[145]

What is reasonably necessary is determined on a case by case basis, and the courts will take into account other funds and income streams available to the beneficiary of the plan.[146] Debtors who are skilled, well-educated, and have

---

[144] A plan is ERISA-qualified if it contains an anti-alienation provision. IRC § 401(a)(13).

[145] Cal. Code Civ. Proc. § 704.115(e).

[146] *In re Bernard*, 40 F. 3d 1028, 1032–1033 (9th Cir. 1994) (annuity did not meet the reasonably necessary standard for an individual, age 60, who earns in excess of $200,000 a year, where he was also entitled to income from other sources upon retirement, including social security

time left until retirement are usually afforded little protection under the California statute as the courts presume that such debtors will be able to provide for retirement.[147]

Contrast California law with protection afforded to IRAs by Florida. Florida exempts all tax-exempt retirement plans from creditor claims, including IRAs.[148]

D. Final Thoughts

The goal of any asset protection plan is to remove the debtor from the title to his assets but in such a way so that it would be difficult to challenge as a fraudulent transfer, would allow the debtor to retain indirect control and the beneficial enjoyment of the assets, and have no or minimal tax consequences. Having gained the understanding of this basic tenet of asset protection, one can focus on analyzing various structures to determine their efficacy.

There are literally dozens of different structures, of varying complexity and sophistication, used by asset protection practitioners to accomplish these goals. The foundational structures covered in this article are a good starting point. Remember that the proper analysis of any asset protection structure is always two-fold: how does the structure work

---

and pension benefits); *In re Spenler*, 212 B. R. 625 (9th Cir. BAP 1997) ($275,000 IRA was not "necessary" where 55-year-old physician who worked approximately 80-90 hours per week could save for his retirement out of his estimated $250,000 annual income).

147 *In re Moffat*, 119 B. R. 201 (9th Cir. BAP 1990), aff'd, 959 F2d 740 (9th Cir. 1992) (practicing orthodontist did not need annuity for support).

148 Fl. Stat. § 222.21(2)(a).

from a theoretical standpoint, and how does it work from a practical standpoint.

We frequently hear the critics of asset protection challenge either the very premise of protecting ones' private property on ethical or social grounds, or challenge the use of a specific structure without suggesting an alternative approach. George and Marilyn cannot be included in that group. When you are faced with the prospect of losing your entire life-time savings, thoughts of ethics and magic bullet structures recede. Your only concern is to preserve at least some of the wealth you had worked so hard to accumulate.

IV. Planning in the Context of Marriage

A. Overview

1. Introduction

With respect to property ownership by spouses, all states follow one of two legal systems: common law or community property.

In **common law states**, as a general rule, property acquired by a spouse prior to marriage, and property acquired during marriage and titled in the name of one spouse, is treated as the separate property of that spouse. Creditors of the debtor spouse cannot reach the separate property of the non-debtor spouse, with the limited exception for necessities of life.

In **community property states**, most property acquired during marriage is treated as community property. Even if property so acquired is titled in the name of one spouse, that merely creates a rebuttable presumption as to the community or separate nature of such property. Because each spouse has a coextensive ownership interest in community property, creditors of either spouse can reach all community property of the two spouses.

2. Common Law Jurisdictions

Most states in the United States follow the common law. In a common law state, property titled in the name of one spouse is treated as the separate property of that spouse. This means that **(i)** only the titled spouse has control over that property; **(ii)** the titled spouse can gift such property without the consent of the other spouse; and **(iii)** only the creditors of that spouse can reach his or her separate property. The separately titled property of the non-debtor spouse is not liable for the debts of the debtor spouse.

Example: Major Nelson is married to Jeannie and they own a house in Coco Beach, Florida. The house is titled in Major Nelson's name. If Jeannie is sued, the house is unreachable by her creditor, because it is titled in Major Nelson's name, and is his separate property.

Planning in a common law state is relatively straightforward in light of the above rule. If between the two spouses one is high-risk (likely to get sued because of the spouse's profession or the business the spouse is engaged in) and the other is low-risk (unlikely to get sued), as much of the couple's property as possible should be titled in the name of the low-risk spouse. Accordingly, if one spouse is a demolition contractor and the other grows roses, most of the couple's property should be titled in the name of the green-thumbed spouse.

However, on divorce, the treatment of the spouses' property is different. All property acquired during marriage,[149] regardless of how it is titled, is treated as marital property,[150] and is subject to a division on divorce.

The distinction that exists in common law states between what property is reachable by a creditor during marriage and subsequent to a divorce is very important. To summarize, during marriage, the creditor can reach only the property titled in the name of the debtor spouse. However, on divorce, all marital property will be divided, regardless of how it is titled and may become reachable by a creditor.

Example: If Napoleon is on title to the Elba farm in upstate New York, then Josephine's creditors cannot reach the farm. However, if the farm was acquired during marriage and is thus marital property, when Josephine divorces Napoleon and is awarded a 50% interest in the farm, her creditors can now reach that 50% interest. Thus, in a common law state the timing of a divorce becomes of great importance.

In a common law state, there does not appear to be any disadvantages in titling the bulk of a couple's assets in one spouse's name. During marriage, the assets are not exposed to the creditors of the high-risk spouse, and on divorce the property will be divided based on its classification as marital or nonmarital, and not based on how it is titled.

A creditor's inability to pursue the non-debtor spouse extends to all separate assets of the spouse, including prop-

---

[149] Other than by gift or inheritance.

[150] Generally, in a common law state, marital property will be any property owned by a spouse except: (i) property acquired prior to marriage; (ii) property acquired during marriage by gift or inheritance; and (iii) property designated as nonmarital through an agreement between spouses.

erties and earnings. It also, generally, does not matter how the liability arose, whether through a spouse's tort or a contractual obligation. Only when the debtor spouse acted as an agent for both spouses, can the non-debtor spouse's property be reached.

3. Community Property Jurisdictions

a. Overview of Community Property

In a community property state there are two types of property: separate and community.[151] Separate property is acquired in much the same manner as in common law states: **(i)** property acquired prior to marriage; **(ii)** property acquired during marriage by gift or inheritance; and **(iii)** property acquired during marriage but as to which the spouses entered into an agreement treating it as separate property.[152]

Separate property in a community property state is afforded similar treatment to separate property in a common law state. During marriage, a creditor of one spouse cannot reach the separate property of the other spouse. However, the one important distinction is that in a community property state, separate property is separate for all purposes, in-

---

[151] There is actually a third form of property in a community property state: quasi-community property. Quasi-community property is real and personal property, wherever it is located, that would have been community property had the spouse been domiciled (resided) in California when he or she acquired it, or any property acquired in exchange for such property. Quasi-community property is treated as community property for liability allocation purposes.

[152] California Family Code Sections 770(a) and 850(a).

cluding divorce. Recall, that in common law states separate property may also be marital property, subject to an equitable division on divorce.

Community property is a form of joint ownership of property by husband and wife. It is defined as real or personal property, wherever situated, acquired by a married person during the marriage while domiciled in this state. Each spouse can manage, direct and control community property.

The distinctive feature of community property[153] is that both spouses own coextensive interests in all of community property. This means that a creditor of one spouse can reach all the community property of the spouses. California Family Law Code Section 910(a) provides:

> Except as otherwise expressly provided by statute, the community estate is liable for a debt incurred by either spouse before or during marriage, regardless of which spouse has the management and control of the property and regardless of whether one or both spouses are parties to the debt or to a judgment for the debt.

The liability of community property extends to contracts entered into by either spouse during marriage, to torts of either spouse during marriage, and to most pre-marriage obligations of either spouse.

---

[153] Community property states include: Alaska, Arizona, California, Idaho, Louisiana, Nevada, New Mexico, Texas, Washington and Wisconsin.

Example: Arnold marries Maria in California, where they continue to live. Prior to marriage Arnold's assets include two barbells and one bottle of body oil. During marriage, Arnold works as an actor and makes $100. Maria's uncle Ted is killed in a drunk-driving accident and leaves her a set of fine china. The spouses have no pre- or post-nuptial agreement.

The two barbells and the bottle of oil are Arnold's separate property. The set of fine china is Maria's separate property. The $100 is community property. If Maria is ever sued, her creditor would look to satisfy its judgment against the set of fine china and $100.

An exception is carved out for earnings of a spouse, which are not liable for pre-marital liabilities of the other spouse.[154] The earnings remain protected even after paid to the non-debtor spouse, provided that the earnings are deposited into a separate bank account.

b. Characterization of Community Property

i. Generally

The five major factors affecting characterization of property as separate or community are the following: **(i)** time of the property's acquisition; **(ii)** the source of funds used to acquire the property; **(iii)** whether spouses entered into a "transmutation agreement" to change the character of property from community to separate, separate to community, and from the separate property of one spouse to the

---

[154] California Family Code Section 911(a).

separate property of the other spouse; **(iv)** actions by parties, including actions that "commingle" or combine separate and community property; and **(v)** operation of various legal inferences, called "presumptions," that help to determine the character of property.

ii. Timing of Acquisition

The most important factor to consider is the timing of the acquisition. Property owned by a spouse before marriage, as well as rents and income from such property, is separate property of that spouse, unless the spouses entered into an agreement to transmute such separate property into community property.

A community property interest can be created only during marriage.[155] Absent an agreement to the contrary, all property, real or personal, acquired during marriage will be treated as community property.

iii. Source of Funds

- **Tracing**

When the timing of the acquisition is unclear or not overly helpful in the analysis, other factors must be taken into account in determining the character of property.

---

[155] For this purpose, marriage ends with a divorce, or, if earlier, when the spouses are legally separated and are living apart (the "separate and apart" test). Spouses are considered to be living "separate and apart"' from each other when they have come to a parting of the ways with no present intention of resuming marital relations, and in which there is conduct evidencing a complete and final break in the marital relationship.

The source of funds used to acquire property of a spouse may help determine the character of such property. This stems from the rule that changing the form of the property does not change its character. For example, if a spouse has a bank account before marriage (treated as separate property), then if the spouse uses the funds in that account to acquire a real estate parcel, such parcel will also be separate property.

If property is acquired during marriage with both community and separate property funds, then there is a presumption that such property is community property. That is based on the general presumption that property acquired during marriage is community property. However, this presumption may be overcome by tracing to the separate property funds, and allocating at least a portion of the property to the separate property interest.[156]

- **Commingling**

For purposes of characterizing property as separate or community, "commingling" means mixing or combining separate and community property into one aggregate. Characterizing commingled property usually requires "tracing" the separate and community contributions back to their respective sources. The mere commingling of separate with community property does not destroy the character of either, provided that their respective amounts can be ascertained.

---

[156] If such property is titled in the name of both spouses, then the community property presumption with respect to such property cannot be overcome by tracing. More concrete evidence will be required to establish a separate property interest.

If property is commingled to such an extent that tracing will not successfully establish its source, then the community property presumption (for property acquired during marriage) cannot be overcome.

The most common type of commingling that takes place during marriage involves commingling separate and community funds in a common bank account. There are two ways to trace such commingled property.

Under the ***direct tracing*** method, a spouse may trace funds in a commingled account to separate property by maintaining a set of itemized, chronological records reflecting all the deposits and the withdrawals from the account. Using such records, it should be possible to establish how much separate property of either spouse went into the account, how much community property went in, and how much separate and community property was withdrawn.

It is important to note that it is not sufficient to simply show the availability of separate funds, the expenditure must be traced back to the source of funds. For example, if Lucy buys property during marriage and titles it in her name alone, it is not enough for her to show that she had separate property funds available for the purchase. To overcome Ricky's claim that the purchased property is community, Lucy will have to demonstrate that she not only had separate funds available, but that separate funds were used to purchase the property.

Example: Lucy and Ricky reside in Hollywood and have a bank account with a balance of $30,000. The balance is the result of Ricky receiving a $20,000 gift from his friend Fred (gifts are separate property), and the remaining $10,000 are the community property earnings of the spouses. Ricky uses $12,000 from the account to purchase a drum. Lucy and Ricky decide to divorce. The drum is community property. Ricky cannot trace the funds used to purchase the drum to his separate property funds. Even though Ricky's records show that there was $20,000 of available separate property funds in the account, Ricky cannot show that these funds were actually used to purchase the drum. Thus, because the property is acquired during marriage, it is presumed to be community property.

The other way to trace commingled funds is through the use of the so-called ***family expense tracing*** method. This method works off the legal presumption that family expenses are paid from community funds. This means that if one spouse can establish that all of the community funds in an account were expended to pay for family expenses, then necessarily, the only funds left in the account are separate property funds. However, the family expense tracing method will work only if the spouse maintained sufficient records to trace deposits and withdrawals from the account, and if the community did not generate sufficient earnings to pay for its expenses.

Example: Ron and Nancy open a bank account and deposit $10,000 in community funds. Ron later deposits $5,000 of separate property funds. During the year, the couple spends $12,000 from the account on family expenses. At the end of the year, Ron spends $500 from the account to buy a saddle. The saddle is Ron's separate property, because of the presumption that community property is used first to pay for family expenses.

To avoid the problems posed by commingling, spouses are always advised to: **(i)** execute and record a separate property inventory that includes all separate property owned at the time of execution; **(ii)** keep financial records adequate to establish the balance of community income and expenditures at the time an asset is acquired with commingled property; or **(iii)** avoid commingling altogether and maintain a separate bank account for separate property funds.

- **Improving Separate Property**

If the spouses use community property funds to improve the separate property of one spouse, that does not change the nature of the separate property. The funds expended by one spouse for the improvement of the separate property of the other spouse are presumed to be a gift between spouses (gifts are always separate property).

However, if one spouse used community property funds to improve his or her own separate property without the consent of the other spouse, the community is entitled to a reimbursement.

- **Acquiring Property with both Kinds of Funds**

When property is acquired during marriage using both separate and community property funds, then, if it is possible to trace, the property will be partially separate and partially community. If tracing is unavailable, then the regular community presumption will apply,[157] and the property will be treated as community property.[158]

---

[157] California Family Code Section 2581. This presumption provides that property acquired during marriage, regardless of how it is titled, is presumed to be community.

[158] However, even if tracing is unavailable, in certain circumstances, separate property may be entitled to a reimbursement of its contribution. See, California Family Code Section 2640.

If property is acquired during marriage with a separate property down payment, and with a loan where the lender relies on the earnings of both spouses, then the loan is community, and thus a portion of the property is separate (the portion attributable to the down payment) and the rest is community. The character of property acquired by a sale on credit or by a loan depends on the intention of the seller or lender to rely on the separate property of the purchaser or to rely on community assets for satisfaction of the debt. The proceeds of an unsecured loan made on the personal credit of either spouse are regarded as community property. Funds borrowed by the pledge of a spouse's separate property are that spouse's separate property. Absent evidence that a seller or creditor relied primarily on the purchaser's separate property in extending credit, the property purchased or money borrowed is presumed to be community property. This result follows the general rule that property acquired during marriage is community property.

For property acquired during marriage, it is important to establish not only the actual amounts of separate and community contributions, but also their respective proportions. Thus, when the property appreciates in value, it will be still possible to apportion.

- **Pursuing a Separate Business**

When one spouse devotes time during marriage to develop his or her separate business and the business appreciates in value, then a portion of that appreciation is attributable to the community. During marriage the time of each spouse belongs to the community, and the time expanded on a separate business is community's time. California courts have established complicated formulas to apportion the appreciation in value between separate property and community property.

iv. Transmutation

Married persons may, by agreement or transfer, and with or without consideration, change or "transmute" the character of their property in any of the following ways: (i) from community property to separate property of either spouse; (ii) from separate property of either spouse to community property; (iii) from separate property of one spouse to separate property of the other spouse.[159]

To be effective, a transmutation agreement must be in writing, the spouses must fully disclose their properties to each other, and a transmutation of real property will be effective as to third-party creditors only if it is recorded.[160]

The law of fraudulent transfers applies to transmutation agreements.[161]

v. The Community Property Presumption

There is a legal inference, called a "presumption," that all property acquired during marriage by either husband or wife or both is community property.[162]

The general community property presumption specifically applies to the following types of property:[163] **(i)** all

---

[159] California Family Code Section 850.
[160] California Family Code Sections 852(a) and (b). See, also, Estate of MacDonald, 51 Cal. 3d 262 (1990).
[161] California Family Code Section 851.
[162] California Family Code Section 760.
[163] *Id.*

real property, including leased property, that is located in California and is acquired during marriage by a spouse while domiciled (living with intent to remain) in California; **(ii)** all personal property, wherever located, that is acquired during marriage by a married person while domiciled in California; and **(iii)** all community property transferred by husband and wife to a trust pursuant to Family Code Section 761.

However, the general community property presumption that property acquired during marriage is community property may be overcome by evidence that the disputed property is actually separate property.

Evidence that may be used to overcome the community property presumption includes the following: **(i)** an agreement between the parties to change the character of (transmute) the property from community to separate property; **(ii)** tracing property to a separate property source; or **(iii)** reliance on separate property as collateral when property is purchased on credit.

If the community property presumption cannot be overcome, the party who has made traceable separate property contributions to the acquisition of property may obtain reimbursement in certain circumstances.[164]

There are several statutory exceptions to the general presumption that all property acquired during marriage is community property: **(i)** property acquired by either husband or wife by gift, will, or inheritance;[165] **(ii)** property that either spouse acquires with the rents, issues, or profits

---

[164] California Family Code Section 2640.
[165] California Family Code Section 770.

from separate property; **(iii)** property held at death and that a spouse acquired during a previous marriage if that marriage was terminated by dissolution more than four years before death; **(iv)** any real or personal property interest acquired by the wife by written instrument before January 1, 1975; **(v)** property acquired by either spouse after separation, unless the property is acquired with community property funds; **(vi)** property designated as separate by a transmutation agreement; **(vii)** personal injury damages paid by one spouse to the other spouse if the cause of action arises during marriage; and **(viii)** personal injury damages received by one spouse from a third party after a court renders a decree of legal separation or a judgment of dissolution of marriage.[166]

vi. Effect of Title on Community Property

- **Joint Tenancy and Tenancy in Common**

The general community property presumption applies to all property acquired during marriage, including property titled in joint form, such as joint tenancy or tenancy in common. A spouse intending to rebut the community property presumption for jointly titled property may do so in one of two ways: **(i)** a clear statement in the deed or other documentary evidence of title by which the property is acquired that the property is separate and not community property; or **(ii)** proof that the spouses have made a written agreement that the property is separate property.

---

[166] See, Family Code Sections 770, 781, 802 and 803.

Neither tracing, nor an oral or implied agreement, is sufficient to rebut the general community property presumption.[167]

Example: Mary and George buy a house during marriage and take title as joint tenants. George uses separate property funds to make the down payment on the house. The spouses make no written agreement that each of their joint interests would be separate property. The remaining payments are made with community funds. The spouses then terminate their marriage. On dissolution, the house will be presumed to be community property. This presumption cannot be overcome because there is no written agreement that the property will be separate. George, however, is entitled to reimbursement for his separate property down payment provided that he can trace the down payment to his separate property funds.

As elsewhere with the community property presumption, it arises only on divorce, and does not affect the spouses' ability to hold property as joint tenants, and does not affect the ability of a third party creditor in reaching the property.

What happens when spouses jointly set up a living trust, and one spouse contributes separate property? While trusts usually provide that they do not alter the separate-community nature of the assets, real estate should always be titled to make it clear that it is either community or separate property. Consequently, the following method of titling is recommended: John and Jane Doe, Trustees of the Doe

---

[167] However, traceable separate property contributions may be reimbursable.

Family Trust dated 1/1/05, as the separate property of Jane Doe.

- **Husband and Wife**

Property titled in the spouses' names as husband and wife creates a community property presumption, unless the instrument indicates otherwise. However, unlike the joint tenancy presumption which is effective only on divorce, the presumption created by the "husband and wife" title is effective both on divorce and against a third party creditor.[168]

- **Property Purchased in Name of Other Spouse**

When a spouse uses either community or his or her separate funds to purchase property in the name of the other spouse alone, there is a presumption, that the purchasing spouse has made a gift of his or her interest (community or separate) to the other spouse.[169] However, the purchasing spouse may attempt to rebut this presumption with evidence that he or she did not intend to make a gift. The rebuttal will be successful if the purchasing spouse establishes **(i)** the separate nature of the funds used to purchase the property, and **(ii)** the existence of an understanding between spouses that the property is not a gift.

---

[168] See, Abbett Electric Corp. v. Storek, 22 Cal. App. 4th 1460, 1466-1467 (1994) (designation of parties as joint tenants, in addition to designation as "husband and wife," showed "different intention," in action by third party creditor); Estate of Petersen 28 Cal. App. 4th 1742, 1747 (1994) (when title held as "husband and wife, as joint tenants," joint tenancy form of title rebuts community presumption arising from "husband and wife" title).

[169] See, In re Marriage of Frapwell, 49 Cal. App. 3d 597, 600-601 (1975).

B. Available Planning Techniques

1. Premarital Agreements

a. Generally

Agreements made in contemplation of marriage between intended spouses and between intended spouses and third parties have been variously described as marriage settlements, marriage contracts, premarital contracts, premarital agreements and antenuptial agreements. For ease of reference, this outline will refer to such agreements as premarital agreements.[170]

Under the Uniform Premarital Agreement Act (adopted by California in 1986), a premarital agreement, to be valid, needs to comply with the following requirements: **(i)** be in writing; **(ii)** be signed by both parties; **(iii)** be voluntarily entered into and not otherwise unconscionable or made without required disclosures of property and financial obligations; and **(iv)** have a lawful object, which may include any of the following matters: **(a)** the rights and obligations of each of the parties in any of the property of either or both of them, whenever and wherever acquired or located; **(b)** the right to buy, sell, use, transfer, exchange, abandon, lease, consume, expend, assign, create a security interest in, mortgage, encumber, dispose of, or otherwise manage and control property;

---

[170] See also, California Family Code Sections 1500 *et. seq*. (general provisions governing marital agreements), and 1600 *et. seq*. (Uniform Premarital Agreement Act).

(c) the disposition of property on separation, marital dissolution, death, or the occurrence or nonoccurrence of any other event; **(d)** the making of a will, trust, or other arrangement to carry out provision of the agreement; **(e)** the ownership rights in and disposition of the death benefit from a life insurance policy; **(f)** the choice of law governing the construction of the agreement; and **(g)** any other matter, including the parties' personal rights and obligations, not violating public policy or a statute imposing a criminal penalty.[171]

Under no circumstances may a premarital agreement affect the child support rights of a child.[172]

A premarital agreement may be revoked or amended only by a written agreement.[173]

Spouses often seek to set aside a premarital agreement, or argue that the agreement is not enforceable as to them. Generally, for a spouse to set aside a premarital agreement, the spouse must demonstrate undue influence, usually coupled with misrepresentation.[174]

To determine the existence of undue influence, the courts will usually attempt to ascertain the parties' respective bargaining power. Some of the factors that the courts will consider include: **(i)** extreme disparities between the parties in age, knowledge, or sophistication; **(ii)** substantial differences between the parties in their respective degrees

---

[171] Family Code Section 1612(a).
[172] Family Code Section 1612(b).
[173] Family Code Section 1614.
[174] Prior to marriage, the soon-to-be spouses do not owe each other fiduciary obligations. The fiduciary obligations of fair dealing and good faith arise only on marriage.

of business expertise; **(iii)** vulnerability of the party claiming undue influence at the time the agreement was executed due to illness, poverty, pregnancy, or similar circumstances; or **(iv)** lack of representation for the party claiming undue influence by independent counsel during the preparation, drafting, and signing of the premarital agreement, especially when the other party was represented.

Previously, premarital agreements that sought to limit spousal support payments on dissolution of marriage were held to be unenforceable, as against public policy (they were sought to promote dissolution of marriage). However, in somewhat recent California Supreme Court case, the Court held that spouses may limit support payments to each other during marriage or on dissolution.[175]

Note: Premarital agreements (as well as the postnuptial agreements discussed below), are legally enforceable documents. That means that in the event of a divorce, the court will respect the division of property agreed to by the spouses in such an agreement. (Thus, the wife may transfer most of her assets to her husband and avoid her creditors, only to find that at some later date her husband files for divorce and gets to keep all assets.)

Consequently, clients must always be warned about this risk when entering into a premarital or a postnuptial agreement. When contemplating entering into such an agree-

---

[175] In re Marriage of Pendleton & Fireman, 24 Cal. 4th 39 (2000). The waiver will be effective when the parties are "intelligent, well-educated persons, each of whom appears to be self-sufficient in property and earning ability, and both of whom have the advice of counsel regarding their rights and obligations as marital partners at the time they execute the waiver."

ment, specifically a postnuptial agreement, the spouses should carefully consider the strength of their marriage union, and weigh not only the possibility of a divorce, but also the likely division of property on divorce.

b. Use in Asset Protection

As the above summary of the California community property laws suggests, holding assets in a community property form is less desirable than separate property, at least from an asset protection perspective. The reason is that all of community property is liable for the debts of either spouse, whether incurred before or during marriage. Contrast that with separate property, which is only liable for the debts of that spouse who owns the separate property (except for obligations with respect to necessities of life).

Clearly, in the context of asset protection planning, one would always want to convert community property to separate. One way of accomplishing that goal is for spouses to transmute their community property into separate. (Transmutation agreements were briefly discussed above, and will be addressed in more detail below.) However, transmutation agreements are subject to the fraudulent transfer laws. In light of that, premarital agreements are a much better way of converting community property into separate.

Example: Fred and Wilma fall in love and decide to get married. Wilma, afraid of losing Fred, forgets to mention to him that she owes a large sum of money to the Bedrock Tax Authority. The couple gets married and lives off Fred's earnings, Wilma is a housewife. The Bedrock Tax Authority proceeds to collect the tax liability from Wilma. Wilma considers filing an offer in compromise, but realizes that Fred's earnings are sufficient to pay off the liability. Because Bedrock is a community property jurisdiction, Fred's earnings can be used to satisfy Wilma's tax liability. The spouses considered entering into a transmutation agreement, but realized that in light of an existing tax liability, the transmutation agreement would probably be a fraudulent transfer.

Fred and Wilma should have entered into a premarital agreement. Why?

Parties to a premarital agreement are generally permitted under the Uniform Premarital Agreement Act to waive property rights that they might otherwise acquire in the future as a result of marriage.[176]

Additionally, the California Supreme Court has suggested that a premarital agreement providing that the spouses' earnings will be their separate property is valid as against subsequent creditors with a right to community funds, provided that no creditor is misled to his or her detriment by the failure of the spouses to inform the creditor that the supposed community assets on which the creditor relied in extending credit are in fact separate assets.[177] See section C. below about recording premarital agreements.

This means, that if Wilma waived her rights to Fred's earnings by using a premarital agreement, Wilma could have filed an offer in compromise. (Prior to marriage, spouses have no interests in each other's property, and Wilma's waiver of future rights is not a transfer for fraudu-

---

[176] California Family Code Section 1612.

[177] In re Marriage of Dawley, 17 Cal. 3d 342, 357 (1976).

lent transfer purposes. As there is no transfer, there is no fraudulent transfer.)

A waiver of property rights through a premarital agreement will be enforceable only if the spouses understood the nature of the rights they were waiving. That is why it is usually recommended that a detailed inventory of assets be attached to a premarital agreement.

It is important to note that certain rights cannot be waived through a premarital agreement, because such rights can only be waived by spouses. An example is a joint and survivor annuity under ERISA.

To a certain extent, premarital agreements may be also challenged as violating the fraudulent transfer laws. For example, if the premarital agreement not only addresses the property rights upon marriage, but also transfers the separate property of one spouse to the other spouse, without property consideration, such transfer may be deemed as being fraudulent as to the present creditors of a spouse.

It should be also noted that transfer of separate property through a premarital agreement is subject to the gift tax, as the parties are not yet married at that time.

c. Recording a Premarital Agreement

Premarital agreements may be executed and acknowledged or proven like a grant of realty and subsequently recorded in each county in which real property affected by the agreement is located; but acknowledgment, proof, and recordation are not required as such for the agreement to be enforceable.[178] Recording or non-recording of a premarital agreement has the same effect as recording or non-recording of a grant of real property.

An unrecorded instrument is valid between the parties and those third parties who have notice of the instrument.[179] Accordingly, an unrecorded premarital agreement is valid as between the spouses. It may also be valid as to third parties who have actual notice of the terms of the agreement. This appears to be the rule, regardless of whether the subject matter of the agreement is real property, personal property, or a combination of the two.

This means that a premarital agreement entered into for asset protection purposes should be recorded to the extent it concerns real property. If the agreement is not recorded, a creditor dealing with one spouse may assume that all of the spouses' property acquired during marriage will be available to satisfy the debt. Consequently, the creditor should be put on notice that this is not the case.

Because spouses usually would not want to disclose to the world all of their financial interests and business dealings, practitioners would often record a document known as a Memorandum of Premarital Agreement. The memorandum is a brief summary of the premarital agreement that does not contain the inventory of spouses' assets, other than real property. The ownership of real property is always a public record.

---

[178] California Family Code Section 1502.
[179] California Civil Code Section 1217.

Some practitioners record the premarital agreement with the full inventory, but deleting the values of the assets. Liabilities never need to be listed.

Even if the creditor was not put on notice as to the fact that there is no community property, or that assets that would ordinarily be community are in fact separate, the creditor can disregard the premarital agreement only if both spouses signed the contract giving rise to the debt. If only one spouse signed, then even if the creditor was not aware of the existence of a premarital agreement, the creditor is precluded from proceeding after the separate property of the non-debtor spouse.

2. Postnuptial and Transmutation Agreements

a. Postnuptial Agreements

An agreement between spouses after the marriage ceremony and affecting the spouses' property rights is referred to as a postnuptial agreement. A transmutation agreement is a postnuptial agreement that changes the character of the spouses' property from community to separate, or vice versa.

Postnuptial agreements are governed primarily by the California Family Code Sections 721, 1500 and 1620. Section 721 provides that postnuptial agreements (as opposed to premarital) are subject to the general rules governing fiduciary relationships that control the actions of person occupying confidential relations with each other.

Section 1500 provides general authority for spouses to alter their property rights by a marital property agreement.

Section 1620 states that, except as otherwise provided by law, a husband and wife cannot, by a contract with each other, alter their legal relations except as to property.

As discussed below, postnuptial agreements that are transmutation agreements are subject to certain other statutory provisions.

b. Transmutation Agreements

i. Generally

Many postnuptial agreements have as their purpose the change, or transmutation, of the character of the parties' property from separate to community, or vice versa. Spouses are free to alter the character of property in this manner, provided that all statutory requirements are met. A transmutation agreement may be used to change the character of property to be acquired in the future, as well as property that the spouses own at the time of the agreement.[180]

The principal limitation on transmutation agreements between spouses is that **(i)** they must be fair and based on full disclosure of the pertinent facts, and **(ii)** they must not be a fraudulent transfer of assets.

The following are the major considerations pertaining to transmutation agreements: **(i)** except for certain interspousal gifts, transmutations of real or personal property are not valid unless made in writing by an express declaration that is made, joined in, consented to, or accepted by the spouse whose interest in the property is adversely affected; **(ii)** transmutations may be made with or without consideration;

---

[180] California Family Code Sections 850, *et. seq.*

(iii) transmutations of real property are not effective with respect to third parties without notice of the transmutation, unless the transmutation is recorded (see, Recording Premarital Agreements, above); **(iv)** transmutations are subject to the laws governing fraudulent transfers; and **(v)** a statement in a will of the character of property is not admissible as evidence of a transmutation of the property in any proceeding commenced before the death of the person who made the will.

ii. Tax Effects

Transmutation agreements have certain tax implications. For income tax purposes, if spouses file a joint return, then characterization of property as community or separate is irrelevant, as all income is aggregated. However, if spouses file a separate return, then each spouse must report his or her one-half share of community income, and his or her separate income. Because transmutation agreements change the nature of the property (including earnings and other income), they have the greatest income tax impact on separate tax returns.

Transfers of property between spouses are generally nonrecognition events for income tax purposes, as they are always considered to be gifts with basis carryover. There are a couple of exceptions: **(i)** transfer to a spouse who is a nonresident alien at the time of the transfer; **(ii)** transfer in trust, to the extent that the sum of the liabilities assumed, plus the liabilities to which the property is subject, exceeds the total adjusted basis of the property; or **(iii)** transfer in trust, of an installment obligation.[181]

The more important tax aspect of a transmutation agreement is the effect that it has on basis step-up (or step-down) at death.

On a spouse's death, one-half of the community property belongs to the surviving spouse, and the other half belongs to the decedent.[182] If the property has appreciated in value during the time that it was held, the entire property will receive a stepped-up basis equal to its fair market value on the date of the deceased spouse's death, if the decedent's half of the property was included in his or her estate.[183] The surviving spouse will receive a stepped-up basis in his or her half of the property, and will therefore have a smaller gain on disposition of that property.

By comparison, if the spouses had held the property separately in joint tenancy with a right of survivorship, the surviving spouse would automatically receive his or her half of the property by operation of law through the original joint tenancy title, and not through inheritance or any other type of succession after death. Consequently, his or her basis would not be stepped up if the property has appreciated, but instead would remain at the original cost basis.

Thus, while transmutation agreements are generally desirable from an asset protection standpoint, they may have adverse tax consequences, because of the loss of one-half of basis step up. By carefully coordinating the transmuta-

---

[181] See, Code Section 1041.
[182] California Probate Code Section 100.
[183] Code Section 1014(b)(6).

tion agreement with the spouses' will or trust, many of the adverse tax consequences can be minimized or eliminated. For example, if the spouses' residence is the separate property of the surviving spouse, then while the residence will not receive a step-up in basis, up to $250,000 of gain will be sheltered on the sale of the residence.

It is important to remember that the loss of the basis step up on one-half of property is important only if it is anticipated that the surviving spouse will be selling his or her separate property. Thus, if the surviving spouse retains her separate assets and sells the property inherited from the decedent (which received a basis step up), no adverse tax consequences will result.

The practitioner should also keep in mind that spouses may enter into a transmutation agreement at any time during marriage. Accordingly, while the spouses are working or practicing their profession (and they are exposed to risks) they can enter into a transmutation agreement and transfer certain assets to the low-risk spouse. When the spouses retire and risks dissipate, the spouses can enter into another transmutation agreement and convert their separate property back to community, regaining the full step up.

While postnuptial agreements are generally subject to the same notice and recording rules as premarital agreements, the rules for transmutation agreements are slightly different.

A transmutation of real property is not effective with respect to third parties who are without notice of the transmutation unless the transmutation instrument is recorded.[184]

---

[184] California Family Code Section 852(b).

While recording is not a prerequisite to the validity of the transmutation as between the spouses, it is a prerequisite in making the transmutation effective with respect to third parties who are otherwise without notice. This requirement is consistent with the fact that transmutations are subject to the laws governing fraudulent transfers.

iii. Structuring the Transmutation Agreement

When clients are first apprised of the uses of transmutation agreements their first impulse is to transfer all the assets to the low-risk spouse. While this impulse is logical, transmutation agreements are subject to fraudulent transfer laws. This means that when assets are divided between spouses pursuant to a transmutation agreement, the division should be on a somewhat equal basis. Approximately 50% of net fair market value of the assets should go to each spouse.

While this practice minimizes the fraudulent transfer likelihood, now only 50% of the assets are protected, and not 100%. However, the usability of the transmutation agreement can be buttressed by allocating "desirable" assets to the low-risk spouse and the "undesirable" assets to the high-risk spouse. In this context, desirable and undesirable is evaluated from a creditor's point of view.

Example: Mrs. Curie is a physics professor at Cal Tech, and Mr. Curie is a plastic surgeon. Mr. Curie gets sued by patients on a bi-weekly basis (he is the high-risk spouse) and Mrs. Curie has never been sued and will probably never get sued (she is the low-risk spouse). The assets of the two spouses are: the medical practice valued at $1 million and a house valued at $1 million. How should the transmutation agreement divide these assets?

The transmutation agreement should make the medical practice the separate asset of the husband and the house the separate asset of the wife. From a creditor's standpoint, the house is a desirable asset (easy to collect against), and the medical practice is an undesirable asset (no value to the creditor other than receivables). Consequently, while the allocation is on a 50-50 basis (each spouse gets an equivalent amount of assets), the asset that is easy to collect against has been moved to the low-risk spouse (where the asset is unreachable by the creditor of the high-risk spouse).

Accordingly, when Mr. Curie is sued again by one of his patients, the patient can collect only against the medical practice, and not against the house.

3. Divorce

a. Common Law States

For spouses planning a divorce, the timing of the divorce can be an effective asset protection tool.

In common-law jurisdictions, a creditor can proceed only after the debtor spouse, and only if the debtor spouse has property vested in his or her name. This means that if pursuant to the divorce the debtor spouse will vest in certain assets, divorce should be postponed, if possible. As soon as the assets are vested in the name of the debtor spouse, the creditors of the debtor spouse will be able to reach such assets.

By the same logic, if the debtor spouse is currently vested in certain assets that are desired by the creditor and divorce would vest such assets in the nondebtor spouse, divorce should be accelerated. Pursuant to the divorce the assets will be transferred from the debtor spouse to the nondebtor spouse, and thus outside of the reach of creditors.

In most common law jurisdictions, marital property is divided equitably on divorce, but not necessarily equally. "Equitably" means that the court is allowed to take a host of factors into account in allocating property between the spouses, such as the respective incomes, ages, health and future income potential of the two spouses. This means that if the two spouses are planning to divorce while minimizing their exposure to creditors of either spouse, the spouses should consider both the timing of the divorce and the division of property on divorce. While the division of property should always be undertaken at arm's-length, certain amount of flexibility is allowed to make the division "equitable."

b. Community Property States

In most community property states, the general rule is that community property can be seized to satisfy community debts even after a divorce. This means that once the community incurred a debt, both spouses are liable for that debt, even following a divorce, and even if the liability has been allocated entirely to only one spouse.[185]

---

[185] Wikes v. Smith, 465 F. 2d 1142, 1146 (9th Cir. 1972).

However, in California, this rule has been changed so that community property awarded to a nondebtor spouse as separate property is protected from the claims of his or her ex-spouse's creditors, even if the debts are community debts. This means that a community debt, which is generally an obligation of both spouses, can be assigned to only one spouse, in California.[186]

With respect to the separate property of spouses following a divorce, the allocation and division of liabilities on divorce in California are as follows:[187]

> **1.** Separate property owned by a married person and property received by that person pursuant to the division of property is liable for debts incurred by the person before or during marriage whether the debt is assigned for payment by that person or that person's spouse.
>
> **2.** Separate property owned by a married person at the time of the division and other property received by that person is not liable for debts incurred by the person's spouse before or during marriage and the person is not liable for such debt unless it was assigned to him or her in the division of property.
>
> **3.** Separate property and other property received by a married person is liable for debts incurred by the person's spouse before or during marriage and the person is personally liable for the debt if it was

---

[186] California Family Code Section 2551.
[187] California Family Code Section 916(a).

> assigned for payment by the person pursuant to the division of property.

While a community debt can be assigned to only one spouse (in California), that does not mean that the spouses can assign all of the liabilities to one spouse, and all of the assets to the other spouse. Transfers of property pursuant to a divorce, like any other transfers of property, are subject to the fraudulent transfer laws.

For example, in Britt v. Damson,[188] the spouses divorced and the husband filed for bankruptcy. There was a claim that the property transferred to the wife pursuant to the divorce was fraudulent. The court held that although the division of property was not fraudulent under state law, it could be under the Bankruptcy Code's fraudulent conveyance provisions. The court stated:

> To the extent that the value of the community property ordered to [the wife] was offset by the value of the community property awarded to husband, the 'transfer' to [the wife] was, as a matter of law, supported by 'fair consideration,' …
>
> To the extent that the award of community property to [the wife] may have exceeded half of the total value of the community property, there is a question whether, under all the circumstances, [the husband] received fair consideration as a matter of law.

[188] Britt v. Damson, 334 F. 2d 896, 902 (9th Cir. 1964), cert. denied, 379 U. S. 966 (1965) .

The Ninth Circuit thus made it apparent that even on divorce, transfers of property can be scrutinized and tested under the fraudulent transfer laws.

In a more recent case, the California Supreme Court attempted to harmonize California Family Code Section 2551 and the UFTA.[189] As discussed above, Section 2551 provides that the property received by a person on divorce is not liable for debt incurred by the person's spouse before or during marriage, and the person is not personally liable for the debt, unless the debt was assigned pursuant to the divorce to that person. This means that in California, divorce overrides the asset protection disadvantages of the community property system.

In contrast to Section 2551 is the UFTA which provides that any transfer of property is subject to the laws of fraudulent conveyances.

The California Supreme Court reasoned that the California Legislature has a general policy of protecting creditors from fraudulent transfers, including transfers between spouses. Just as the fraudulent transfer laws apply to transmutation agreements during marriage, so do those laws apply to transfers of property on divorce.

Despite the court's holding the transfers of property on divorce are subject to the UFTA, challenges under the UFTA are still limited in the context of divorce and leave room for planning opportunities. Under the UFTA, a creditor can allege that the transfer was either actually or constructively fraudulent.

---

[189] Mejia v. Reed, 31 Cal. 4th 657 (2003).

Constructive fraud requires little more than a finding that one of the spouses was left insolvent—a straight forward and objective analysis. However, actual fraud requires a subjective analysis which makes it more difficult for a creditor to prevail in the context of divorce. Courts are most reluctant to delve into the inner thoughts of spouses in an attempt to discern the intentions behind a divorce.

V. Use of Trusts in Asset Protection

The goal of all asset protection planning is to insulate assets from claims of creditors without concealment or tax evasion. It is usually impossible to completely and absolutely protect assets, and the focus is on making assets more difficult and more expensive to reach.

All asset protection planning is based on the following two premises: **(1)** creditors can generally reach any asset owned by a debtor;[190] and **(2)** creditors cannot reach those assets that the debtor does not own.[191]

When working within the context of the first premise, the goal is to make it more difficult and more expensive for a creditor to reach the debtor's assets. This may include encumbering assets, converting assets from non-exempt to exempt, substituting assets or transferring ownership to legal entities. Working within the second premise, the goal is to fit within its parameters, but without any detriment to the client-debtor. Generally, this means that as the end-result of the planning, the debtor should not own any assets, but should retain their beneficial enjoyment and some degree of control.

Continuing with the second premise, debtors strive to achieve two incompatible goals: **(i)** they want to possess the beneficial enjoyment or control of their assets, whether through direct ownership or otherwise, and **(ii)** they also

---

[190] Code of Civil Procedure § 695.010(a).
[191] *Id.*

want to distance themselves from the ownership and control over the assets, to make such assets inaccessible to creditors.

In this obvious dichotomy, trusts come to the rescue by splitting the beneficial enjoyment of trust assets from their legal ownership.

The beneficiaries of a trust are the beneficial owners of the assets holding equitable interests, but they do not hold legal title to the assets. The legal title is vested in the trustee of the trust. The trustee of a trust thus stands in the position of a fiduciary to the beneficiaries.[192] The trustee holds title to the trust assets for the benefit of the beneficiaries and has to administer the trust for the benefit of the beneficiaries and no one else.[193]

A creditor's ability to satisfy a judgment against a beneficiary's interest in a trust is limited to the beneficiary's interest in such trust.[194] Consequently, the common goal of asset protection trusts is to limit the interests of beneficiaries in such a way so as to preclude creditors from collecting against trust assets.

Trusts are widely used in asset protection. Not all types of trusts are effective asset protection devices, but a properly drafted and structured trust may be an almost impregnable form of asset protection.

---

[192] See, generally, Probate Code §§ 16000-16015.

[193] Probate Code § 16002(a).

[194] *Garcia v. Merlo* (1960) 177 Cal.App.2d 434; *Booge v. First Trust & Sav. Bank* (1944) 64 Cal.App.2d 532-536; *Estate of Bennett* (1939) 13 Cal.2d 354.

A. Structuring Trusts for Asset Protection

1. Revocable v. Irrevocable

a. Generally

The most commonly drafted trust is the revocable inter-vivos trust (the so-called "living trust"). Living trusts protect beneficiaries from claims of creditors to the same extent as irrevocable trusts. However, if the debtor is a settlor of the trust, the living trust will not provide the settlor-debtor with any measurable degree of asset protection, because of and to the extent of the settlor's power to revoke.[195]

The protective benefits of an irrevocable trust were addressed in a recent California decision, *Laycock v. Hammer.*[196] In 1998 the debtor established an irrevocable life insurance trust and a few months later transferred a life insurance policy to the trust. A couple of years later the debtor (and then his estate) was pursued on a money judgment and the creditor attempted to reach the life insurance policy transferred to the irrevocable trust. The court stated unequivocally that the life insurance policy was the property of the trust and not of the debtor, and the creditor could not reach the policy.[197]

Consequently, any trust created to protect the assets of a settlor must be irrevocable.

---

[195] Probate Code § 18200.
[196] (2006) Cal.App.4th (slip opinion).
[197] Slip. Opn. page 9.

Practice *Pointer*: A living trust may have a very limited asset protection use. A living trust that has a generic name (*i.e.*, instead of the Jane Smith Trust, the Sunshine Trust), and a third-party trustee, can be used to own real property, and will afford the settlor a certain amount of anonymity. A creditor of Jane Smith will have a more difficult time ascertaining what real estate she owns if the real estate is titled in the name of the third-party trustee of the Sunshine Trust. This type of planning has limited usefulness: **(i)** if the debtor's name appears anywhere in the chain of title (a diligent search will pull up the property), and **(ii)** because a title company may refuse to insure the sale of the property if it knows of the connection between the debtor and the trust.

b. The Qualified Personal Residence Trust

The qualified personal residence trust ("QPRT") is an irrevocable trust very frequently used for both estate planning and asset protection. QPRTs are used to transfer a settlor's residence out of the settlor's estate at a low gift tax value. Once the trust is funded with the settlor's residence, the residence and any future appreciation of the residence is excluded from settlor's estate.

The QPRT is a split-interest trust, with the settlor retaining a term-of-years right to live in the residence rent-free, with the remainder interest going to the remainder beneficiaries. The gift of the remainder interest is a completed transfer, and the settlor no longer owns that interest and it is not reachable by the creditors of the settlor.

To the extent the settlor retains an interest in the QPRT, the QPRT will be deemed self-settled (discussed below), and the protective benefits of the trust will not apply. However, even though a settlor's creditor has the legal ability to reach the retained interest, in practice that is rarely, if ever, attempted. The retained interest has very little value to a creditor because such an interest would be difficult to sell at a foreclosure sale.

Consequently, creditors either do not pursue residence interests held in QPRTs, or are more willing to negotiate on favorable terms with the settlor-debtor.

2. Spendthrift Trusts

a. Generally

A spendthrift trust is a type of trust that either limits or altogether prevents a beneficiary from being able to transfer or assign his interest in the income or the principal of the trust.[198] Spendthrift trusts have traditionally been used to provide for beneficiaries who are incompetent or are simply unable to take care of their own financial affairs. Today, almost every trust incorporates a spendthrift clause.

<u>Example</u>: Mr. Howell is worried that his wife will spend her entire inheritance on a shopping spree in Paris. Instead of giving her unfettered access to the trust on his death, the trust provides that the trustee shall make periodic distributions of cash to Mrs. Howell. Mrs. Howell is not

---

[198] *County Nat. Bank etc. Co. v. Sheppard* (1955) 136 Cal.App.2d 205; 11 Witkin, *Summary of Cal. Law* (9th ed. 1990) Trusts, § 165, p. 1017.

given any power to invade the trust or anticipate her distributions (no power to transfer or assign interest in the trust).

If a trust incorporates a spendthrift clause and the beneficiary is therefore precluded from transferring his interest in either income or principal, then the beneficiary's creditor will not be able to reach the beneficiary's interest in the trust.[199]

The protection of the spendthrift trust extends solely to the property that is in the trust. Once the property has been distributed to the beneficiary, that property can be reached by a creditor, except to the extent the distributed property is used to support the beneficiary.[200] If a trust calls for a distribution to the beneficiary, but the beneficiary refuses such distribution and elects to retain property in the trust, the spendthrift protection of the trust ceases with respect to that distribution and the beneficiary's creditors can now reach trust assets.[201]

b. Exceptions to the Spendthrift Protection

There are three notable exceptions to the protection afforded to a beneficiary of a spendthrift trust.

---

[199] Code of Civil Procedure § 695.030(a) and Probate Code §§ 15300 and 15301(a).
[200] Probate Code §§ 15300, 15301(a), 15306.5(c); *Frazier v. Wasserman* (1968) 263 Cal. App. 2d 120, 127.
[201] Probate Code § 15301(b).

i. Self-Settled Trusts

If the settlor of a trust is also a beneficiary of a trust, then the assets that the settlor has retained a benefit in will not be protected by the trust's spendthrift clause.[202] This is known as a prohibition against "self-settled" trusts.

The settlor does not need to be either the sole settlor or the only beneficiary of the trust. As long as the settlor is a beneficiary of the trust to any extent, to that extent the trust will be deemed self-settled.

Example: Husband and wife establish a trust for their own benefit and contribute their community property. The trust will be self-settled as to each spouse.

Example: John settles a trust for the benefit of his children but retains for himself the right to income for life. To the extent of John's retained lifetime income interest, the trust is self-settled. The remainder interest for the benefit of children is not self-settled, as the children-beneficiaries were not settlors.

If a trust is self-settled that means only that the interest of the settlor-beneficiary is not protected from creditors. It does not mean that the trust is invalid, that other beneficiaries are unprotected or that the trust does not offer other benefits. In the above example, the trust is self-settled only as to John, and not as to his children.

The prohibition against self-settled trusts in California is well-settled. In *DiMaria v. Bank of* California *Natl. Assoc.*,[203] the settlor-beneficiary of a trust retained the right to the income for life and to invade principal if income was

---

[202] Probate Code § 15304(a).
[203] (1965) 237 Cal.App.2d 254.

insufficient for her support, with remainder interest given to her children. The trustee was required to make distributions pursuant to an ascertainable standard. The settlor could not revoke the trust.

The court held that only "the income and the additional corpus required for her support and obtainable by her from the trustee" is subject to creditor claims.[204] The rest of the corpus, including the remainder interest were not for the benefit of the settlor-beneficiary, and thus not self-settled (and therefore not reachable by the settlor's creditors).

If the trustee of a self-settled trust has any discretion in making distributions, then the creditors of the settlor may reach the maximum amount that the trustee may distribute in his discretion to the settlor-beneficiary.[205]

Consequently, when a trust is self-settled, to obtain any asset protection for the settlor, discretionary powers should be avoided in favor of a clearly ascertainable standard.

While California, like most other jurisdictions, strips the spendthrift protection of a trust when it is self-settled, certain jurisdictions no longer conform to this rule. These jurisdictions include certain U.S. states, like Delaware, Alaska and Nevada, and certain foreign nations, like Saint Vincent and the Grenadines and the Cook Islands (these jurisdictions are discussed in more detail, below). Forming an irrevocable trust in one of these jurisdictions may be another way to preserve the protection of the spendthrift clause of a self-settled trust.

---

[204] *Id.* at 258.
[205] Probate Code § 15304(b).

ii. Sole Trustee and Sole Beneficiary

When a debtor is the sole beneficiary and the sole trustee of a trust, the trust's protective benefits are lost because the trust is deemed terminated and the beneficiary holds trust assets free of trust.[206] This happens because of the doctrine of merger—the debtor now holds all the equitable interests in the trust in his capacity as the beneficiary and all the legal interests in his capacity as the trustee. When the equitable and legal interests are vested in one person, there is no longer a trust relationship and that person can fully dispose of the property as any other person.

California has a limited anti-merger statute which provides that when the settlor of a trust is also the sole trustee and the sole beneficiary, the trust is not merged or terminated if it names one or more successor beneficiaries.[207] The intent of this statute is to insulate a trustee of living trust from personal liability when acting in his capacity as a trustee.[208]

Because the California anti-merger statute has little relevance when drafting asset protection trusts, such trusts should not have the same one trustee and beneficiary. This may be avoided by naming a co-trustee, by adding another beneficiary, or by picking a jurisdiction with a strong anti-merger statute.

---

[206] *Hill v. Conover* (1961) 191 Cal.App.2d 171, 180; *Ammco Ornamental Iron, Inc. v. Wing* (1994) 26 Cal.App.4th 409, 417; Rest. 2d Trusts § 99, subd. (5), com. e., pp. 228-229.
[207] Probate Code § 15209(a).
[208] *Mead v. Dickinson* (2004) 2004 Cal.App.Unpub.LEXIS 5657, page 20.

A beneficiary of a trust includes any person who has a present or future interest in the trust, vested or contingent.[209] In *Ammco Ornamental Iron,* a creditor of a beneficiary, who was also the sole trustee, attempted to challenge the spendthrift clause of an irrevocable trust by arguing that under the doctrine of merger the trust terminated. The debtor-beneficiary held a life estate, and on his death the trust corpus was to be distributed to the beneficiary's children pursuant to a testamentary power of appointment held by the beneficiary. The court held that when the remainder beneficiary is in existence and ascertained, and the remainderman's interest is not subject to a condition precedent, the remainder interest is vested in such beneficiary.[210] The fact that the interest of the remainder beneficiary was subject to a complete divestment (due to lifetime distributions to the current beneficiary), did not change the remainder beneficiary's status as a beneficiary of the trust.[211] Consequently, the children of the debtor-beneficiary also qualified as the beneficiaries of the trust, and the doctrine of merger was inapplicable.

iii. Support Payments

Even if an irrevocable trust has a spendthrift clause, a court may order the trustee to satisfy a beneficiary's support obligation to a former spouse or minor child out of any distributions that the trustee has decided, in his discretion, to make to the beneficiary.[212]

---

[209] Probate Code § 24(c).
[210] *Ammco Ornamental Iron* at 418.
[211] *Id.*
[212] Probate Code § 15305(c).

This is an example of two conflicting public policy rationales. Spendthrift clauses have been enforceable, historically, because our society places a great deal of importance on private property rights. Consequently, creditors cannot generally reach a beneficiary's interest in a spendthrift trust. However, our society places an even greater importance on satisfying support obligations, and even a spendthrift trust will not shield a beneficiary from such obligations.

3. Discretionary Trusts

a. Generally

A trust is called "discretionary" when the trustee has discretion (as to the timing, amount and the identity of the beneficiary) in making distributions.[213] There must not be any trust provisions that mandate a distribution, but there may be provisions that set standards for distributions.[214] Because the trustee is not required to make any distribution to any specific beneficiary, or may choose when and how much to distribute, a beneficiary of a discretionary trust may have such a tenuous interest in the trust so as not to constitute a property right at all. If the beneficiary has no property right, there is nothing for a creditor to pursue. The statutes follow this line of reasoning by providing that a trustee cannot be compelled to pay a beneficiary's creditor

---

[213] 11 Witkin, *Summary of Cal. Law* (9th ed. 1990) Trusts, § 166, p. 1019.

[214] Probate Code § 15303(c).

if the trustee has discretion in making distributions of income and principal.[215]

Practice Pointer: When drafting a trust that allows the trustee to exercise discretion in making distributions subject to a standard (including an ascertainable standard), the discretion clause should be carefully worded. Practitioners should always favor using permissive phrases such as "trustee may pay to the beneficiary" instead of mandatory phrases such as "trustee shall pay to the beneficiary." In *U.S. v. Taylor*,[216] the trust provided that the trustee "shall pay" to the beneficiary so much of the income from the trust as the trustee deemed necessary for the support of the beneficiary. The court interpreted that language to mean that the trustee was mandated to make distributions, and his discretion was limited only to determining the amount "necessary."[217]

Even if a trust is truly discretionary it should have a spendthrift clause. While the trustee would not need to honor a beneficiary's demand for a distribution, it is possible that absent the spendthrift clause a creditor would force the beneficiary to assign his interest in the trust (whatever it may be) to the creditor. If that happens, then some day when the trustee does make a distribution, it will be made to the creditor. Also, most trusts are never fully discretionary, and it makes sense to obtain the protection of the spendthrift clause.

---

[215] Probate Code § 15303(a).
[216] (N.D. Cal. 1966) 254 F.Supp. 752.
[217] *Id.* at 755.

Once the beneficiary receives a distribution from the trust, even if it is discretionary, the protective benefits of the trust cease. The distributed assets are treated as any other assets of the beneficiary-debtor, and there is no statutory protection available for such assets simply because the assets used to be held in a trust.

In a case of first impression, a California court held that even a fully discretionary trust cannot shield a beneficiary from child-support obligations because of the overriding public policy support for satisfying child support obligations.[218] In interpreting Probate Code § 15305, the court stated that "The statute cannot have been intended to allow a beneficiary to defraud support creditors by hiding behind the trustee's discretion."[219]

The court's analysis is suspect. The intent of the Probate Code is irrelevant if the debtor-beneficiary has no property right in the trust because of a trustee's unfettered discretion.

b. Drafting Considerations

A properly drafted discretionary trust is an almost impregnable form of asset protection. But if the trust is discretionary, it means that there are no mandated distributions and no demand rights granted to the beneficiary. This potentially leaves the beneficiary at the mercy of the trustee.

---

[218] *Ventura County Dept. of Child Support Serv. v Brown* (2004) 117 Cal.App.4th 144.
[219] *Id.* at 155.

To some extent beneficiaries are protected from the trustee by statutes. Trustees must always exercise their discretion reasonably, and even if the trustee is granted "sole and absolute" discretion, the discretion must not be exercised "arbitrarily" and must be exercised in accordance with fiduciary principles.[220]

The statutes are not sufficient to ensure that the beneficiary will receive either regular or demanded distributions when not threatened by creditors, and it is up to the practitioner to carefully draft the trust to achieve that goal while maintaining the asset protection benefits of the trust.

4. Drafting Trusts for Maximum Protection and Control

a. Distribution Standards

The protection of a discretionary trust is not diminished by setting forth a distribution standard for the trustee.[221] This allows the drafter to build into the trust some protection for the beneficiary, from the trustee, by including some broadly defined standards. Including distribution standards in an asset protection trust is not always advisable, as in a case of a foreign asset protection trust. Because foreign trusts are usually established for debtors facing greater creditor exposure, protecting beneficiaries from creditors is more important that protecting them from the trustee. In

---

[220] Probate Code §§ 16080 and 16081(a).
[221] Probate Code § 15303(c).

these cases, distribution standards are usually sacrificed in favor of unfettered discretion.

When a distribution standard is desired, the following sample standard may be used:

> The trustee may, in its discretion, pay to or apply for the benefit of the beneficiary, so much of the income or principal of the trust as the trustee deems advisable to provide for the beneficiary's health, support, comfort, maintenance, education, professional or vocational courses, and to otherwise enable the beneficiary to maintain his accustomed standard of living. The trustee may also pay to or apply for the benefit of the beneficiary so much of the income or principal of the trust as the trustee deems advisable to allow the beneficiary to purchase a residence, a business or to make investments.

b. Stated Intent

It is also advisable to set forth in the trust the settlor's intent for the trust. The courts in California have consistently held that it is the court's duty to carry out the intent of the settlor, provided it does not violate public policy.[222] The intent can be stated in terms of providing for and taking care of the beneficiary, and not paying any monies to

---

[222] *Brock v. Hall* (1949) 33 Cal.2d 885, 889.

any party other than the beneficiary, including the beneficiary's creditors.

c. Balancing Control and Protection

Striking the right balance between surrendering the ownership of trust's assets and retaining some control over and benefit from such assets is a difficult task. From control perspective, the debtor-beneficiary wants to be either a trustee of the trust, or wants to impose mandates and standards on the third-party trustee. From an asset protection perspective, the debtor-beneficiary needs a spendthrift trust with the maximum possible discretion conferred on the trustee.

When the debtor-beneficiary is the sole trustee of a discretionary trust, he has unfettered access to the assets of the trust. As discussed above, if the debtor is the sole beneficiary of the trust and also the sole trustee, then under the doctrine of merger the trust, regardless of its form, will not provide the debtor with any protection. Consequently, it may be advisable to add a co-trustee, or to add remainder beneficiaries.

In practice, some practitioners appoint the sole beneficiary as the sole-trustee of a discretionary, spendthrift trust, and provide for an automatic removal of the beneficiary as a trustee if, and when, he becomes a debtor. The hope is to accomplish the best of both worlds, give the beneficiary complete control over trust assets when there are no creditors pursuing the beneficiary, and to promptly remove the beneficiary as a trustee and achieve asset protection when the creditors appear. If the beneficiary is truly the sole beneficiary of the trust (*i.e.*, there are no remainder or contingent beneficiaries) at any time, then under the doctrine of merger the trust terminates. It is not clear what happens when a new trustee is substituted or a co-trustee is added, as there is no trust in existence at that time. Similar to the advice above, practitioners should consider adding a friendly co-trustee (possibly with limited powers) or remainder beneficiaries at the outset.

d. Protecting Mandatory Distributions

No matter what distribution standards are drafted into the trust or how much control is given to the beneficiary, some settlors may want mandatory distributions. A mandatory distribution provision in a trust does not take into account the discretion of the trustee. The trustee simply must make the distribution in the manner and at the time prescribed in the trust (an example of a mandatory distribution includes a QTIP trust, where income must be paid to the surviving spouse on a quarterly basis). Mandatory distributions present a problem because sometimes the trustee may be required to make a distribution when a beneficiary is being pursued by a creditor.

If a trust calls for mandatory distributions and the protection of the beneficiary is desirable, it may be advisable to include in the trust a clause prohibiting any and all distributions to a beneficiary while that beneficiary is being pursued by a creditor.[223] It is important to make clear the settlor's intent that such clause should override all other trust provisions.

B. Domestic Asset Protection Trusts

A properly drafted trust, incorporating the pointers from the discussion above, may be an insurmountable obstacle to creditors; provided that the trust is for the benefit of a third-party beneficiary.[224] Most asset protection clients are looking to protect their own assets and are usually not beneficiaries of existing trusts. Consequently, the majority of asset protection trusts are self-settled. Because California strips the spendthrift protection of a self-settled trust, practitioners must look to other jurisdictions.

Several U. S. jurisdictions now allow self-settled trusts to afford their settlors the protection of the spendthrift clause. Alaska was the first jurisdiction to enact such laws in 1997[225] and was shortly followed by Delaware,[226] Nevada[227] and a few others.[228] All of these domestic self-settled asset protection trusts shall be referred to as "DAPTs."

---

[223] N.B. This may be inadvisable in a QTIP trust, because it will then fail to qualify for the unlimited marital deduction.

[224] The protective benefits of a trust may also be lost pursuant to a fraudulent transfer challenge. Civil Code §§ 3439-3439.12. A discussion of fraudulent transfers is beyond the scope of this article.

[225] Alaska Statutes § 34.40.110.

[226] 12 Del. Code § 3572 (Qualified Dispositions in Trust Act).

[227] Nev. Rev. Stat. ch. 166.

[228] Mo. Ann. Stat. § 428.005 *et. seq.*; R.I. Gen. Laws §§ 18-9.2. Oklahoma allows *revocable* self-settled trusts, and prevents creditors from forcing the settlor to exercise his power to revoke. 31 Okla. Stat. Ann. §§ 13, 16.

Using Delaware as sample DAPT jurisdiction, a Delaware DAPT must comply with the following requirements: **(i)** the trust must be irrevocable and spendthrift; **(ii)** at least one Delaware resident trustee must be appointed; **(iii)** some administration of the trust must be conducted in Delaware; and **(iv)** the settlor cannot act as a trustee.[229]

The DAPT jurisdictions appear to be a simple solution for a settlor of a self-settled trust seeking asset protection if the settlor is a resident of a DAPT jurisdiction and has assets in the jurisdiction. California residents with California assets may not be able to reap the asset protection benefits of these trusts.

1. The Risks of DAPTs

a. Conflict of Law

Trusts are generally governed by the laws of the jurisdiction that is designated by the settlor as the governing jurisdiction.[230] There are two exceptions to the general rule: **(i)** states will not recognize laws of sister states that violate their own public policy,[231] and **(ii)** if the trust owns real property, such property will be governed by the law of jurisdiction that is the property's situs.[232]

---

[229] 12 Del. Code § 3570.
[230] Rest. 2d Conf. of Laws § 273(b); Uniform Trust Law § 107(1).
[231] *Washington Mutual Bank v. Superior Court* (2001) 24 Cal.4th 906, 916-917; Rest. 2d Conf. of Laws § 187, subd. (2); Uniform Trust Law § 107(1).
[232] Rest. 2d Conf. of Laws § 280.

In determining whether a law of another state would be enforceable in California, the court would analyze whether the law of the other state is contrary to a fundamental policy of California, and would then determine whether California has a "materially greater interest" than the other state in adjudicating the issue.[233]

To date, there are no California (or any non-DAPT jurisdiction) cases dealing with the protectiveness of DAPTs. It is possible that if a case involving a DAPT was litigated in California, the California court may not recognize the law of the DAPT jurisdiction and refuse to extend the spendthrift protection to a self-settled trust.

If a DAPT owns California real property, then California law will govern any collection action applicable to the real property and the spendthrift protection of the DAPT jurisdiction will be inapplicable.[234] This problem may be remedied to some extent by having a DAPT own California real estate through a limited liability company or a limited partnership organized under the laws of the DAPT jurisdiction. This way the trust no longer owns California realty, but owns an intangible governed by the laws of the DAPT jurisdiction.[235]

b. The Full Faith and Credit Clause

The Full Faith and Credit clause of the Constitution provides that each state has to give full faith and credit to the

---

[233] *Washington Mutual Bank* at 916.
[234] Rest. 2d Conf. of Laws § 280.
[235] Corporations Code §§ 15691, 17450(a).

laws of every other state.[236] This means that if a California court refuses to recognize the protection of a DAPT and enters a judgment for the creditor, the creditor may be able to enforce the judgment against the trustee of the DAPT, even if that trustee was located in the DAPT jurisdiction.

However, even under the Full Faith and Credit clause the states are not required to recognize the laws of sister states that are contrary to their own public policy.[237] Consequently, a DAPT jurisdiction court may refuse to enforce a California judgment because it was entered under trust laws substantially different to those of the DAPT jurisdiction.

At this point the analysis becomes quite circular. A creditor argues in California court that the court should apply California law and not Alaska law to an Alaska trust because Alaska trust law violates California public policy against self-settled trusts. In turn, Alaska refuses to recognize the California judgment because it violates Alaska public policy in protecting self-settled trusts.

This analysis should lead the practitioner to one inescapable conclusion. Until the application of the Full Faith and Credit clause is litigated in the context of a self-settled trust, the risk is too great that a DAPT would not afford the debtor with the required protection.

---

[236] U.S. Const., Art. IV, § 1.
[237] *Nevada v. Hall* (1978) 440 U.S. 410, 424.

2. Foreign Trusts – The Superior Alternative

Foreign trusts are discussed in a lot more detail below. This section will simply point out the various aspects that make a foreign trust more advantageous than a DAPT.

The term "foreign trust" usually means a trust that states that it should be interpreted under the laws of a foreign jurisdiction. This means that the laws of the foreign jurisdiction will apply to the trust and the enforceability of the trust's spendthrift clause. What advantages does that carry?

All foreign jurisdictions that compete in the asset protection market allow self-settled trusts to be an effective shield against creditors. This is similar to the U. S. DAPT jurisdictions that have now gone the same route.

However, foreign trusts are not subject to the Full Faith and Credit clause or the Supremacy Clause. This means that with a foreign trust there is never any doubt that the favorable law of the foreign jurisdiction will be applied to the trust, and there is also no doubt that the foreign jurisdiction does not have to enforce any judgment coming out of a U. S. state (whereas a sister state may have to recognize such a judgment).

However, even setting aside this uncertainty, foreign trusts are vastly superior to the Alaska-type trusts. For example, the foreign asset protection jurisdictions provide that the creditor has the burden of proving a fraudulent conveyance. More importantly, the creditor's burden of proof is the criminal standard of "beyond a reasonable doubt."

In foreign jurisdictions the statute of limitations on bringing a fraudulent conveyance action is not only short, but it also begins running on the date of the transfer, not the date the transfer is "discovered."

Finally, while not a legal deterrent, the costs associated with challenging a foreign trust prove to be an insurmountable obstacle to most creditors. It also surprises many that foreign trusts are usually less expensive to set up and administer than DAPTs.

VI. Foreign Trusts

A. Overview

Even if the settlor of a domestic asset protection trust ("DAPT") resides in the DAPT jurisdiction and all the assets of the trust are located in the DAPT jurisdiction, the efficacy of a DAPT may be challenged under the Supremacy clause of the U.S. Constitution, under the applicable fraudulent transfer statute, or because the settlor retained some prohibited control over the trust.

The only possible way of avoiding all these obstacles when planning with trusts is through the means of a foreign trust. A foreign trust, *per se*, does not have any asset protection benefits. The benefits come from the jurisdiction which governs the trust. Several jurisdictions compete in the foreign trust arena and have drafted their trust laws to address all or most of the problems and issues discussed above.

The commonly understood meaning of the term "foreign trust" is a trust governed by the laws of a foreign jurisdiction. However, as discussed below, the term "foreign trust" has a very specific meaning under the Code. Whenever the term "foreign trust" appears in this text, it refers simply to a trust governed by the laws of a foreign jurisdiction.

Foreign trusts are truly efficient for asset protection purposes only if liquid assets are used to fund the trust, and such assets are, at some point, transferred offshore. While a foreign asset protection trust can hold any property, including personal and real property in the U. S., the ability of a U. S. court to reach U. S. property suggests the benefits of holding offshore assets in the foreign trust.

Foreign trusts are usually treated as "foreign trusts" for the purposes of the Code. This means that transfers of assets to the trust will be treated as a sale for tax purposes. To avoid the sale treatment on the funding of the trust, most foreign trusts are drafted as grantor trusts. Being grantor trusts, they avoid sale treatment on funding, and remain tax neutral during their existence. Foreign asset protection trusts are usually established solely for asset protection purposes, and almost never for tax purposes.

Generally, when contrasted with a domestic trust, a foreign trust offers the following benefits:

1. Increased ability of the settlor to retain benefit and control;
2. Less likely to be pursued by a creditor;
3. Foreign jurisdictions usually have more beneficial to the debtor statute of limitations, burden of proof, and other important provisions;
4. No full faith and credit, comity or supremacy clause issues;
5. Favorable to the debtor spendthrift provision laws;
6. Confidentiality and privacy; and
7. Flexibility.

B. Protective Features of Foreign Trusts

Foreign trusts offer two major advantages to debtors. From a practical perspective, because the trustee is domiciled in a foreign nation, at some point in time the creditor would have to litigate its claim against the trustee and pursue a collection action in that foreign nation. That is a costly proposition for all creditors, particularly if the creditor is a plaintiff's attorney who is not licensed to litigate in that foreign nation.

From a legal perspective, several offshore jurisdictions have enacted trust laws that are particularly favorable to debtor-beneficiaries and debtor-settlors. Jurisdictions like the Cook Islands (in the South Pacific),[238] Saint Vincent and the Grenadines (in the West Indies),[239] and Nevis (in the West Indies)[240] are considered to be among the best currently available foreign trust jurisdictions. The trust laws in all three jurisdictions are almost identical, as both Saint Vincent and Nevis based their trust laws on the laws of the Cook Islands. Using Saint Vincent as an example (but all three jurisdictions have similar provisions), the following favorable asset protection provisions have been incorporated into that nation's trust laws: **(i)** there is no recognition of foreign judgments with respect to trusts;[241] **(ii)** there is a very short statute of limitations on fraudulent transfers;[242] **(iii)** to establish a fraudulent transfer the creditor must show that the debtor was insolvent,[243] and must establish

---

[238] Cook Islands International Trusts Act, 1984.

[239] Saint Vincent and the Grenadines International Trusts Act, 1996.

[240] Nevis International Exempt Trust Ordinance, 1994.

[241] See, *e.g.*, Saint Vincent and the Grenadines International Trusts Act, 1996, Part X, § 39.

[242] See, *e.g.*, Saint Vincent and the Grenadines International Trusts Act, 1996, Part XI, § 46.

[243] See, *e.g.*, Saint Vincent and the Grenadines International Trusts Act, 1996, Part XI, § 45(1)(b).

the debtor's intent to "hinder, delay or defraud" beyond a reasonable doubt;[244] **(iv)** the anti-duress provisions are incorporated into the statutes;[245] and **(v)** spendthrift protection is extended to self-settled trusts.[246] These jurisdictions also offer the additional advantages of **(a)** not being subject to the U.S. constitutional issues like the Full Faith and Credit clause; **(b)** using the English common-law legal system; **(c)** having abolished the rule against perpetuities; and **(d)** not allowing trusts to be pierced for child or spousal support.

Not all offshore jurisdictions offer the same asset protection benefits as the three cited above. For example, Bahamas lacks clauses **(i)**, **(ii)** and **(iii)**. Bermuda and Cayman Islands lack clauses **(i)**, **(ii)**, **(iii)** and **(v)**. Mauritius lacks clause **(i)**.

Interestingly, New Zealand has been recently gaining popularity as an asset protection destination. New Zealand is closely tied to the Cook Islands (which were a former New Zealand protectorate) and its trust laws are at the forefront of other developed nations. New Zealand does not tax trusts that generate their income elsewhere, but it does recognize self-settled trusts. In eyes of some practitioners, New Zealand is not a "notorious" asset protection jurisdiction, and makes planning easier.

---

[244] See, *e.g.*, Saint Vincent and the Grenadines International Trusts Act, 1996, Part XI, § 45(5).

[245] See, *e.g.*, Saint Vincent and the Grenadines International Trusts Act, 1996, Part III, § 10(2).

[246] See, *e.g.*, Saint Vincent and the Grenadines International Trusts Act, 1996, Part II § 9(7).

There are several disadvantages to using New Zealand for asset protection purposes. New Zealand has a relatively long statute of limitations on fraudulent transfers (four years), it will recognize a U. S. judgment, and there is no established history of protecting trust settlors and beneficiaries from creditors. (At least not to the same extent as in St. Vincent, the Cook Islands and Nevis.) Because foreign asset protection trusts should be used openly, and they are extremely effective if established in the right jurisdiction, perceptions by creditors (and even judges) are not very important.

The nonrecognition of foreign judgments is the most important protective feature of the offshore asset protection jurisdictions. Assume that a creditor obtains a judgment against a debtor in a California court and would like to enforce the judgment against the debtor's assets. The debtor's assets have been transferred into a Saint Vincent trust which in turn funded a Swiss bank account.[247]

The creditor will be unable to domesticate its judgment in Saint Vincent, and will usually be unable to litigate its case *de novo* in Saint Vincent.[248] Consequently, the credi-

---

[247] Unlike most DAPT jurisdictions (see, *e.g.*, Alaska Statutes § 13.36.035(c)(1)), the foreign trust jurisdictions do not require that the trust hold any assets in the jurisdiction of its domicile. Consequently, a Saint Vincent or Cook Islands trust can hold assets located anywhere in the world.

[248] The creditor will generally be unable to bring a lawsuit against the debtor in Saint Vincent because a Saint Vincent court would not have personal jurisdiction over the debtor. See, generally, *International Shoe Co. v. Washington* (1945) 326 U.S. 310, 316 (if the court does not have personal jurisdiction over the defendant, than minimum contacts must exist between the defendant and the jurisdiction). Additionally, Saint Vincent would not be the proper venue for a lawsuit, because a

tor's sole remedy would be to bring a fraudulent transfer action against the trustee of the foreign trust and attempt to show that the settlement of the trust by the debtor constituted a fraudulent transfer.

Given that the more favorable asset protection jurisdictions have a very short statute of limitation for fraudulent transfers,[249] require proof of intent beyond a reasonable doubt, and require proof of debtor's insolvency, the creditor faces a daunting task.

C. Maximizing Protection of Foreign Trusts

1. Location of Assets

The nearly impregnable asset protection of a foreign trust may only be relied upon if the trust holds foreign assets. If the trust holds U.S. real estate, the jurisdiction over the real estate and the applicable choice of law forum will usually be the jurisdiction where the real estate is located (see above).

For personal property, including intangibles, the choice of law should be the domicile of the foreign trust (see above), but so long as a court in the U.S. has any jurisdiction over the assets, the protection cannot be assured. For

---

lawsuit can be brought in the jurisdiction where the debtor resides, where the cause of action arose, or where the contract was entered into. 15 U.S.C. § 1692i(a)(2)(A)-(B); Code of Civil Procedure § 395(a).

[249] For example, in Saint Vincent, the statute of limitations is two years from the date of the cause of action against the debtor-settlor, or one year from the settlement of the trust. Saint Vincent and the Grenadines International Trusts Act, 1996, Part XI, § 46(1).

example, if the debtor transfers share certificates of a publicly traded corporation to his foreign trust, the judge can disregard the trust or the laws of the foreign jurisdiction applicable to the trust and can then issue an order to the corporation's stock transfer agent to cancel the debtor's shares and issue new shares to the creditor.

The assets of a foreign trust need to be located offshore only when the creditor commences its collection actions against the debtor-settlor. Until such time when the settlor becomes a debtor, the trustee can hold trust assets in the U.S. For fraudulent transfer purposes, the relevant testing date is the settlement of the trust. Where the trust holds its assets, or what those assets are, is irrelevant in the fraudulent transfer analysis. However, because the assets may need to be moved offshore quickly, there is a strong preference for using foreign trusts to hold liquid assets.

2. Drafting Considerations

Foreign trusts are a commonly used asset protection device for two reasons: **(i)** a properly drafted trust should avoid most of the problems cited in the reported decisions (as discussed below), and **(ii)** a foreign trust may be the best available alternative for most debtors, even if "bullet-proof" protection cannot be obtained.

a. Trustee

A very important issue in establishing a foreign trust is the selection of the trustee for the trust. The foreign trustee selected should have no U. S. contacts, directly or indirectly, through affiliates, subsidiaries, agents or representatives. A trustee having any contacts with the U. S., whether directly or through agents, may risk having "minimum contacts"[250] with the U. S., thus becoming subject to the jurisdiction of a U. S. court.

Additionally, it is important to properly characterize trustee's powers in the trust. This is a common dilemma facing settlors. Settlors want to retain control over the trust assets and retain access to the assets, while sufficiently removing themselves from the trust so as not to have any control for the contempt analysis (see below).

This is usually accomplished by the use of a discretionary trust, wherein the trustee has full discretion in deciding when, to whom and how much to distribute from the trust. The discretionary trust is supplemented with a "letter of wishes" which is a non-binding expression of the settlor's intentions. The letter of wishes can advise the trustee on how the settlor would like the trustee to exercise its discretionary powers. Because the letter of wishes is merely a statement of settlor's intent and is not binding on the trustee, it is not treated adversely in the "contempt" analysis. The letter of wishes may be updated on an annual basis.

Settlor may also wish to appoint an independent third party as a trust advisor or a trust protector. The job of this independent (but friendly to the settlor) third party would be to assist the trustee in making decisions with respect to distributions from the trust and other discretionary powers of the trustee.

---

[250] The minimum contacts test is the requisite threshold to establish nexus under the Due Process clause.

Because a trust advisor or a trust protector may be viewed in the same capacity as a trustee, it is inadvisable to have such person in the U. S. unless the advisor's/protector's powers are merely passive. If the powers are passive, meaning the advisor/protector can veto a trustee's decision or remove the trustee, but cannot force or advise the trustee to undertake an action, then such person may reside in the U. S. There would be no power that such advisor/protector possesses that may be used by a U. S. court to the detriment of the debtor.

In a more recent case,[251] the district court was asked by the Department of Justice to determine whether the settlor of a foreign trust, one Arline Grant, had to repatriate the money to pay down her tax liability. Arline Grant's husband was the settlor of two foreign trusts, one in Jersey and one in Bermuda, and she became the sole beneficiary of both trusts on his death. The question before the court was whether Arline Grant was simply a beneficiary or did she possess any control over the trust to make her something more than a mere beneficiary. "Once the power of the person who is either the owner or the beneficiary of the asset to repatriate is established, the court can require that person to repatriate the funds."[252]

Both trusts granted Arline Grant the power to replace the trustee and appoint a new trustee, which could be located anywhere in the world. Her power to appoint a new trustee was absolute and not subject to approval by any other person. Once appointed, the trust would then be governed by

---

[251] U.S. v. Grant, 2005 U.S. Dist. LEXIS 22440 (S.D. Fl. 2005).
[252] *Id.*

the laws of the jurisdiction where the new trustee was located.

The court concluded that it had the power to force Arline Grant to replace the existing trustee with a U.S. trustee, and thus repatriate the funds. The court further concluded that as a practical matter, Arline Grant had the power to ask the existing trustee for a distribution of the trust corpus, and such distribution would not be denied. The court ordered Arline Grant to appoint new trustees for both trusts, each based on the United States, and alternatively, to repatriate the funds to the United States.

Like the Andersons, the Grants had a poorly drafted trust.

b. Contempt

Because California and other U.S. courts are unable to reach the foreign assets of a foreign trust, or exercise jurisdiction over the foreign trustee, the courts focus on the sole person that they can control—the settlor-debtor.

If a California court (that usually would have personal jurisdiction over a California resident debtor) orders the debtor to repatriate the assets of a foreign trust, the debtor may have to obey the court order or be held in contempt.

Contempt is generally defined as an act of disobedience to an order of a court, or an act of disrespect of a court.[253] There are two types of contempt: civil (intent is to coerce a party to do something) and criminal (intent is to punish a

---

[253] *Black's Law Dictionary* 313 (7th ed. 1999).

party for an action).[254] Both types of contempt involve the imposition of similar sanctions: payment of money, imprisonment, or both.[255] However, if the court orders a party to do something that is practically impossible, a civil contempt charge will not stand.[256]

In a foreign trust situation, the court usually attempts to coerce the debtor into repatriating the money, which is civil contempt.[257] The debtor, in turn, tries to establish that it is impossible for him to comply with the court order, and the contempt charge should not stand.[258] A number of cases have attempted this line of attack.

In the most notable case on point, *F.T.C. v. Affordable Media, LLC*,[259] the debtors, who allegedly engaged in a telemarketing fraud scheme, funded a Cook Islands trust and appointed themselves as the co-trustees and protectors of the trust, together with a Cook Islands trust company.

---

[254] *Id.*

[255] In asset protection cases debtors usually have no money, and imprisonment becomes the sole available sanction.

[256] *U.S. v. Rylander* (1983) 460 U.S.752, 757 ("Where compliance is impossible, neither the moving party nor the court has any reason to proceed with the civil contempt action.")

[257] Criminal contempt has a high burden of proof, and usually requires a jury trial. It rarely applies to asset protection cases because criminal contempt cannot be used coercively – *i.e.*, the debtor will spend time in jail regardless of whether any money is retrieved from the trust.

[258] Even if compliance is impossible, contempt charges will stick if the impossibility is self-created. Impossibility will be deemed self-created if the foreign trust is funded in close proximity to the timing of the court's order. *In re Lawrence* (11th Cir. 2002) 279 F.3d 1294, 1300. In *Affordable Media* (see below), the impossibility arose after the court ordered the debtor to repatriate the funds.

[259] (9th Cir. 1999) 179 F.3d 1228 (colloquially referred to as the "Anderson" case).

When the court ordered the debtors to repatriate the assets of the trust, the debtors, acting as co-trustees of the trust, had sufficient control over the trust to repatriate the assets. The debtors, however, notified their Cook Islands co-trustee of the court order, and were promptly removed as a co-trustee. They were held in contempt of court by the district court.

On appeal to the Ninth Circuit the debtors argued that it was impossible for them to comply with the repatriation order because the Cook Islands trustee (by then the sole acting trustee) refused to repatriate the assets. The Ninth Circuit held that the debtors did not demonstrate that it was impossible for them to repatriate the money and upheld the district court's contempt charge.[260] The court then analyzed whether the debtors retained sufficient control over the assets of the trust.

According to the court, the following facts were indicia of control: **(i)** no rational person would send millions of dollars overseas without retaining control over the money; **(ii)** the debtors previously withdrew $1 million from the trust to pay a tax liability; and **(iii)** they acted as a protector of the trust with the ability to remove the Cook Islands trustee and appoint a new trustee.[261]

These arguments appear valid until one revisits the purpose of civil contempt, which is to coerce the debtor to repatriate the assets. All of the arguments made by the court establish that the debtors possibly did have sufficient control, at some point, to repatriate the money. However, once

---

[260] *Id.* at 1240.
[261] *Id.* at 1242-1243.

the debtors surrendered their control, there was no further purpose to the contempt charge.

The court's analysis was also faulty as follows: **(i)** rational people may give up control over their assets if the alternative is to lose the assets to a creditor; **(ii)** even though a debtor may surrender control over his assets, he will still be the beneficiary of the trust holding equitable interests in the assets of the trust; **(iii)** in *Affordable Media,* the debtors withdrew money from the trust when they were co-trustees, but as soon as they were removed as co-trustees that control string was cut; and **(iv)** the fact that a trust may allow the beneficiary to petition for distribution when there is no collection action and removes that power when there is a collection action is simply good practice; it does not establish that control exists at all times.

In the few reported contempt cases, courts appear to be eager to find contempt.[262] One possible explanation is the Ninth Circuit statement in *Affordable Media* that foreign asset protection trusts operate by frustrating the jurisdiction of domestic courts.[263] The court's logic appears to be on very shaky ground. Any transfer to a foreign person or entity, where the debtor does not remain in control over the transferred assets, will frustrate the jurisdiction of a domestic court. The debtor may gift all of his assets to a Mexican corporation, contribute his assets to a U.K. trust, or assign them to a Swiss GmbH. What frustrated the Ninth Circuit were not the debtor's actions or intentions, but the differ-

---

[262] See, *e.g., In re Lawrence,* (Bankr. S.D. Fla. 1999) 238 B.R. 498; *Eulich v. U.S.* (2006) 2006 U.S.Dist.LEXIS 2227.
[263] *Affordable Media* at 1232.

ence in the law among these jurisdictions. With the non-asset protection jurisdictions, a court's judgment may be enforceable in the foreign jurisdiction; the foreign jurisdiction may have more creditor-friendly fraudulent transfer, trust and collection statutes. The only real difference between a debtor funding an Alaska trust and a Cook Islands trust is in the applicable law (including the application of the federal constitutional law), not the debtor's actions.

The debtor's choice of law should not factor into the impossibility analysis. The only question is whether the debtor has retained control over the assets, so that it would not be impossible for the debtor to repatriate the assets (which was the Ninth Circuit's ultimate holding in *Affordable Media*). If there is no finding of control, impossibility exists, and contempt should not stand.

Consequently, a finding of contempt is solely a question of poor drafting. If the trust allows the settlor-debtor sufficient control over the trustee, then the courts are within their right in finding the debtor in contempt, as in *Affordable Media.* But if the debtor has completely surrendered control, contempt charges should not stand. Consequently, foreign trusts should be drafted as arm's-length irrevocable trusts, with spendthrift clauses, and as much discretion as possible conferred on the trustee. Debtors should never act as co-trustees or protectors, or retain any power to remove a trustee and appoint a new trustee.[264]

---

[264] The debtor's power to replace a trustee with a U.S. domiciled trustee caused repatriation of a foreign trust's assets in *U.S. v. Grant* (2005) 2005 U.S. Dist. LEXIS 22440.

c. Best Available Alternative

Foreign trusts may not work 100% of the time; they may be exposed to possible risks and challenges, but for many debtors a foreign trust may be the best available asset protection alternative.

There are approximately twenty reported cases piercing the protective benefits of foreign trusts; some are discussed above. Even assuming that these cases are not due to bad drafting or bad facts, they still represent an infinitesimally small percentage of all foreign trusts. According to a speech delivered by Jack Straw in 2002 (at the time, the British Foreign Secretary), it was estimated that approximately $6 trillion was held in "offshore" structures (and that number is probably higher today).[265] Based on the anecdotal evidence available to the author, approximately 10,000 trusts have been established in the aggregate in the Cook Islands, Nevis and Saint Vincent.

There is a simple reason why foreign trusts are extremely effective the vast majority of the time. Unless the creditor has the deep pockets of an agency of the U.S. government, or of a large bank, it is simply too expensive to pursue the assets of a foreign trust.

---

[265] U.N. Human Rights Report 2002, Annex 1.

D. Tax Treatment

There are two tax implications of foreign asset protection trusts: tax treatment implications and reporting requirements.

1. Foreign v. Domestic for Tax Purposes

In the common nomenclature, the term "foreign trust" means a trust that is governed by the laws of a foreign country. For tax purposes, the term "foreign trust" is a term of art. Pursuant to Code Section 7701(a)(31)(B), a foreign trust is any trust other than a domestic trust. A domestic trust, pursuant to Code Section 7701(a)(30)(E), is a trust that meets both the "court test" and the "control test."

a. Court Test

To meet the court test, a court in the U. S. must be able to exercise primary supervision over the administration of the trust.[266]

The term "primary supervision" means that a court has or would have the authority to determine substantially all issues regarding the administration of the entire trust.[267] Administration includes maintaining books and records, filing tax returns, managing and investing the assets of the trust, defending the trust from suits by creditors, and de-

---

[266] Code Section 7701(a)(3)(E)(i).

[267] Treas. Reg. Section 301.7701-7(c)(3)(iv).

termining the amount and timing of distributions.[268] If both a U. S. court and a foreign court can exercise primary supervision, then the trust will also satisfy the court test.[269]

The regulations provide a safe harbor for the court test. Under the safe harbor, a trust will satisfy the court test if: **(i)** the trust instrument does not direct that the trust be administered outside the U. S.;[270] **(ii)** the trust is in fact administered exclusively in the U.S.; and **(iii)** the trust is not subject to an automatic migration provision.[271]

An automatic migration provision is any trust clause which provides that if a U. S. court attempts to assert jurisdiction or supervise the administration of the trust, the trust would no longer be administered in the U. S., but would now be administered and subject to the laws of a foreign country.[272]

Some practitioners have advocated drafting asset protection trusts that are governed by U.S. law but giving power to a trustee or a third-party to change the governing law of the trust. Thus, the trust would have no automatic migration clause but would still be able to migrate if the circumstances demanded so.

A trust drafted as a domestic trust without an automatic migration clause would certainly satisfy the safe harbor of the regulations. However, if a trustee or a third-party exer-

---

[268] Treas. Reg. Section 301.7701-7(c)(3)(v).

[269] Treas. Reg. Section 301.7701-7(C)(4)(i)(D).

[270] For the purposes of the test, territories and possessions are not counted
as U. S.

[271] Treas. Reg. Section 301.7701-7(c)(1).

[272] Treas. Reg. Section 301.7701-7(c)(4)(ii).

cises the power to migrate the trust offshore, that may be deemed a fraudulent transfer, and the trustee or the third-party may be potentially liable for the fraudulent transfer.

b. Control Test

To meet the control test, one or more U. S. persons must have the authority to control all substantial decisions of the trust.[273]

A U. S. person is defined in Code Section 7701(a) (30) as a citizen or resident of the U.S., or a partnership or corporation organized in the U. S. "Substantial decisions" means those decisions that are not ministerial.[274]

The control test basically requires an appointment of a U. S. trustee or trust protector.

If the trust originally appointed a U. S. trustee and the trustee was later inadvertently substituted with a foreign trustee (which causes the trust to become a foreign trust), the trust is allowed 12 months to rectify that problem by replacing the foreign trustee with a U. S. trustee.[275]

2. Tax Treatment of Foreign Trusts

Pursuant to Code Section 684, a transfer of property to a trust treated as a foreign trust for tax purposes is deemed to be a sale of assets to the foreign trust for fair market value.

---

[273] Code Section 7701(a)(30)(E)(ii).
[274] Treas. Reg. Section 301.7701-7(d)(ii). Ministerial decisions include: bookkeeping, collection of rent and making investment decisions.
[275] Treas. Reg. Section 301.7701-7(d)(2).

This causes the settlor of the trust to recognize gain. Additionally, if a domestic trust is recharacterized as a foreign trust, the domestic trust is treated as selling its assets to the foreign trust.

The only time there will be no gain recognition on the settlement of a foreign trust is when the foreign trust is treated as a grantor trust under the rules of Code Section 671.

In addition to direct transfers of assets to a foreign trust, certain indirect or constructive transfers will trigger gain recognition.

a. Indirect Transfers

Indirect transfers are present when the assets are transferred to the foreign trust through an intermediary. The transfer of property must be made pursuant to a plan "one of the principal purposes of which is the avoidance of U. S. tax."[276]

Tax avoidance will be deemed to be the principal purpose if **(i)** the U. S. person is related to the beneficiary of the foreign trust, and **(ii)** the following conditions are <u>not</u> present:

> **1**. The intermediary has a relationship with a beneficiary of the trust that establishes a reasonable basis for concluding that the intermediary would make a transfer to the foreign trust;

---

[276] Treas. Reg. Section 1.679-3(c)(1).

2. The intermediary acted independently of the U. S. person;
3. The intermediary is not an agent of the U.S. person under generally applicable United States agency principles;[277] and
4. The intermediary must have timely complied with the reporting requirements of Code Section 6048.[278]

The four conditions establish the existence of an arm's-length relationship between the settlor and the intermediary.

If there is a transfer to a foreign trust through an intermediary and one of the principal purposes is tax avoidance, then the existence of the intermediary is disregarded, and the settlor is treated as making a direct, taxable transfer to the foreign trust.[279] The settlor will be taxed on the transfer when the settlor transfers the property to the intermediary, not when the intermediary transfers the property to the trust.

b. Constructive Transfers

The term "constructive transfer" is defined in the regulations as "any assumption or satisfaction of a foreign trust's obligation to a third party."[280] Additionally, a guarantee of

---

[277] The principle test for agency is control.
[278] Treas. Reg. Section 1.679-3(c)(2).
[279] Treas. Reg. Sections 1.679-3(c)(1) and (3).
[280] Treas. Reg. Section 1.679-3(d).

a trust's obligation may be deemed as a transfer to the trust.[281]

The tax effect of the assumption of debt or the guarantee of a liability is taxation of the settlor on the amount deemed transferred.

Additionally, a transfer of property to a foreign entity owned by a foreign trust will be treated as a transfer by the settlor to the foreign trust, followed by a contribution by the trust to the foreign entity.[282]

3. Grantor Trust Rules

a. Classification as a Grantor Trust

The classification of an offshore asset protection trust as a foreign trust is prohibitive from a tax standpoint. Yet, all offshore asset protection trusts are foreign trusts for tax purposes. The sole purpose of an offshore asset protection trust is to change the applicable law to a foreign country and to empower a foreign trustee to administer the trust. Obviously, that has the effect of failing both the court and the control test and both are needed to classify a trust as domestic.

However, even if a trust is classified as a foreign trust, and Code Section 684 taxes transfers to foreign trusts, there is an exception carved out for foreign trusts that are grantor trusts within the meaning of Code Sections 671-679.[283]

---

[281] Treas. Reg. Section 1.679-3(e).
[282] Treas. Reg. Section 1.679-3(f).
[283] Code Section 684(b).

Under the grantor trust rules, a trust will be treated as a grantor trust if the grantor (the settlor) retains a reversionary interest in the trust, has power to control beneficial enjoyment, has power to revoke the trust, may receive income distributions from the trust, or if the trust is foreign and has a U. S. beneficiary.

Generally, most of these conditions will apply to a foreign asset protection trust. However, the last clause, which is contained in Code Section 679 is present in virtually every foreign asset protection trust.

Pursuant to Code Section 679, a foreign trust will be treated as a grantor trust if **(i)** there is a transfer of property to the trust, at a time when **(ii)** the trust has a U. S. beneficiary. A U. S. beneficiary is defined as a U. S. person who is, or may be, a beneficiary of the trust. Thus, even a contingent future U. S. beneficiary of a fully discretionary trust will be treated as a U. S. beneficiary. Even if the trust presently does not provide for any possibility of having a U. S. beneficiary, if the trust may be amended in the future to include a U. S. beneficiary, the trust will be treated as having a U. S. beneficiary.

However, if the interest of a potential beneficiary is remote, that beneficiary will be disregarded. A beneficiary's interest is remote when the likelihood of that person becoming an actual beneficiary is negligible. For example, the regulations give an example of a first cousin who may become a beneficiary under the laws of intestate succession, but the possibility of that happening is so remote that the first cousin is disregarded as a beneficiary.[284] The remote

[284] Treas. Reg. Section 1.679-2(a)(2)(iii), Ex. 7.

interest exception does not apply to the trustee's discretion. This means that so long as the trustee has discretion to select a U.S. beneficiary, the trust will be treated as having a U. S. beneficiary.

In determining the existence of a U. S. beneficiary, attribution rules are applied to corporations and partnerships.

If the trust has a U.S. beneficiary, the transferor is taxed not only on income of the trust during the year, but on all undistributed net income of the trust since it was created.[285]

b. Tax Treatment of Grantor Trusts

The bright side of treating a foreign asset protection trust as a grantor trust under Code Section 679 is the fact that Code Section 684 does not apply. Which means that grantors are free to settle trusts with appreciated property without gain recognition. Treatment as a grantor trust also ensures that the transfer of assets to the trust is not subject to the gift tax (which is usually the primary consideration, as foreign trusts are usually settled with cash and not appreciated assets).

However, if the trust is treated as a grantor trust, that also means that pursuant to Code Section 671, the grantor (settlor) of the trust is taxed on all trust income (settlor of the foreign trust continues to report trust's income on her 1040). This is the reason why foreign asset protection trusts are always tax neutral. They are always treated as grantor

---

[285] Code Section 679(b).

trusts under Code Section 679, and thus do not allow the settlor to escape taxation.

4. Reporting Requirements

a. On Transfer of Assets to the Trust

As a general rule, transfers to foreign trusts have to be reported to the Service.[286] The reporting requirements were revised substantially in 1997, with the issuance of Notice 97-34.[287] Under the Notice, transfers fall into two categories: gratuitous and nongratuitous.[288]

With certain exceptions, gratuitous transfers to foreign trusts have to be reported to the Service on Form 3520. For these purposes, a transfer is gratuitous if it is made for less than full consideration (the transfer does not need to constitute a gift for tax purposes).

Nongratuitous transfers must also be reported to the Service on Form 3520 if no gain is recognized at the time of the transfer of appreciated property, or the transferor is related to the trust.[289]

An exception to the Form 3520 requirement is a fair market value sale to the trust (a "transfer for value"). A transfer for value "includes only transfers in consideration

---

[286] Code Section 6048(a).
[287] 1997-1 C.B. 422.
[288] Notice 97-34, Section III.
[289] Notice 97-34, Section III, D. In this context, a person related to the trust will include the settlor, a beneficiary, or a person related to the settlor or beneficiary.

for property received from the trust, services rendered by the trust, or the right to use property of the trust."[290] A transfer of property to a trust in exchange for an interest in the trust does not constitute a transfer for value.

Additionally, most obligations received by a settlor who transfers money or other property to a "related" trust will not constitute a transfer for value and will be subject to the Form 3520 reporting requirements.[291] There is an exception for "qualified obligations" which will constitute fair market value.

To constitute a qualified obligation, it must meet certain conditions, such as having a term of not less than five years and bearing interest at a rate between 100 percent and 130 percent of the applicable federal rate. To be a qualified obligation, the obligation must be reported to the Service on Form 3520.

Accordingly, it is not possible to avoid the reporting requirement by using obligations. If the obligations are not qualified, then the transfer is gratuitous and Form 3520 must be filed. To make the transfer nongratuitous, the obligation must be qualified by reporting it to the Service on Form 3520.

b. Annually

A return for the foreign trust is required to be filed by the trustee (or agent who is authorized to sign) on Form 3520-A. Copies must then be provided to the grantor and

---

[290] Notice 97-34.
[291] Code Section 6048(a)(3)(B)(i); Notice 97-34, Section III, C.1.

the beneficiaries. However, while the trustee is required to file the return, the obligation to ensure the filing falls on the owner of the trust.[292]

c. Agent

Generally, the trust will appoint a U. S. agent for the limited purpose of accepting service of process with regard to witnesses and books and records pursuant to Code Sections 7602, 7603 and 7604. The U.S. agent "shall not subject such persons or records to legal process for any purpose other than determining the correct" income tax treatment of trust income. Further, the foreign trust that appoints the agent will not be considered to have an office or permanent establishment in the United States or to be engaged in a U.S. trade or business solely because of the agent's activities.[293]

The effect of these rules is to allow the IRS access to the information required for determining tax liability in all events and regardless of the secrecy laws of foreign countries. When a U.S. agent is not appointed, the IRS is authorized to determine the amount of income to be taken into account under the grantor trust rules.

See Notice 97-34, Section IV.B. for form of agent appointment.

d. Reporting by Beneficiaries

A beneficiary of the trust must file Form 3520 if he is a

---

[292] Code Section 6048(b)(1).
[293] Code Section 6048(b)(2)(B).

U. S. person and receives (directly or indirectly) any distribution from the foreign trust during the taxable year.[294]

The reporting requirement applies only if the U.S. person has reason to know that the trust is a foreign trust. The information required includes the name of the trust, the aggregate amount of the distribution received during the year, and such other information that the IRS prescribes. In determining whether the U.S. person receives a distribution from or makes a transfer to a foreign trust, the fact that a portion of the trust is treated as owned by another person under the grantor trust rules is disregarded.

e. Penalties

The penalty for failure to file Form 3520 is 35% of the "gross reportable amount."[295] An additional $10,000 penalty is imposed for a continued failure for each 30-day period, or a fraction thereof, beginning 90 days after the IRS notifies the responsible party of the failure. The total amount of the penalties, however, is limited to the gross reportable amount.

If a portion of the transaction is reported, then the penalty will be imposed only on the unreported amount. An additional 5% penalty is imposed on the failure to comply with the annual reporting requirement.[296]

---

[294] Code Section 6048(c).

[295] Code Sections 6677 and 6039F(c). There is a "reasonable cause" and "not willful neglect" defense available for this penalty.

[296] Code Section 6677(b).

VII. Advanced Planning with Foreign Trusts

A. Offshore Defective Grantor Trusts

1. Defective Grantor Trusts Generally

An installment sale to a defective trust[297] in exchange for the trust's promissory note has become an increasingly popular estate transfer strategy with many significant benefits.[298] Generally, this technique is used to sell non-controlling interests in entities to the trust, while taking advantage of the valuation discounts and freezing the value of the estate.

The trust is drafted as an irrevocable dynasty trust, but intentionally violating one or more of the grantor trust rules under Code Section 671. Most frequently, the trust is made defective for income tax purposes by appointing the grantor as the trustee of the trust.[299] With respect to the appoint-

---

[297] These defective grantor trusts are sometimes referred to as "intentionally" defective grantor trusts. The author believes the word "intentionally" to be redundant, because a trust would not be drafted as defective unless it was intentionally (barring acts of malpractice).

[298] Defective grantor trusts are viewed as being superior to GRATs because there is no requirement that the grantor outlive the trust, and because the GST exemption may be claimed up front.

[299] One planning element commonly incorporated into defective grantor trust is the ability to switch trustees, appointing an independent third party as the trustee. When that happens, the trust ceases being a grantor trust. Likewise, an independent third party trustee can be removed and

ment of the trustee in this setting there is an often exploited distinction between the attribution rules for estate tax and income tax purposes. For example, if the grantor's spouse is appointed as a trustee with the power to sprinkle income among beneficiaries, that power is not attributed to the grantor (but the trust must be funded with the grantor's separate property, not community property of the spouses). However, the powers held by the grantor's spouse is attributed to the grantor for income tax purposes.

The note is typically structured as interest-only, with a balloon payment at the end. The note should bear an adequate rate of interest, determined under Code Section 7872. In Revenue Ruling 85-13, 1985-1 C. B. 184, and several private letter rulings, the Service ruled that the sale of property by the grantor to the trust will be ignored for income tax purposes, because the grantor trust is a disregarded entity.

Because the trust is irrevocable, and is otherwise drafted to be outside of the grantor's estate, the property placed in the trust escapes estate taxation. To ensure this result and prevent the application of Code Section 2036, the grantor should set the trust up for someone else's benefit, *i.e.*, children. To avoid the application of the gift tax, the discounted value of property sold to the trust should equal the fair market value of the note.

Because the anti-freeze rules of Code Section 2702 may apply to a defective grantor trust, it may be advisable to

---

the grantor appointed trustee, with the trust switching back to grantor mode.

pre-fund the trust with assets equal to 10% of the value of the property that will be sold to the trust.

The property within the trust continues to appreciate in value, while the value of the promissory note is fixed (the note earns a constant rate of return that is usually lower than the rate of appreciation of the assets within the trust). The value of the note will be included in the grantor's estate. Leveraging the life-time estate and gift tax exclusion, and by discounting the value of partnership or LLC interests placed in the trust creates significant estate tax savings. Additionally, because income taxes are paid by the grantor and do not constitute a gift to the trust,[300] additional wealth is shifted from the grantor's estate and into the trust.

A defective grantor trust would work particularly well for a start-up business or a new business opportunity. A start-up business, with low initial value but great upside potential, can be transferred to the trust at minimum value, with all the business growth occurring within the trust, and outside the settlor's estate.

As a matter of fact, a business opportunity within a defective grantor trust calls for a slightly different structure to be optimally efficient. Where the trust requires little seed money to start the new business, it is advisable to have a client's parent, sibling or other party seed the trust, with the client named as beneficiary. So long as the client is not treated as the grantor of the trust, Code Section 2036 issues do not arise. The client can then act as the trustee of the trust and will be the primary beneficiary.

---

[300] A discharge of one's legal obligation is not a gift.

As the trust makes interest payments on the note to the settlor, the settlor does not take the payments into income, as the transaction is ignored for income tax purposes. However, it is unclear what happens on the death of the settlor when the trust loses its grantor status, and the payments become taxable. Does the settlor's estate begin to recognize income? The answer is not entirely clear. It has been suggested that on the initial sale the settlor elect out of the installment method, thus accelerating all the gain realization on the sale. However, because at the time of the sale the trust has grantor status, the gain is not actually taxable to the grantor. At the time of death, the argument goes, there is no gain left to recognize. While there is no authority on this point, this strategy may work, and because there is no downside risk, the election out of the installment method should always be undertaken.

It is also possible to pay off the note prior to the settlor's death when the trust still has its grantor status. It is advisable in that case to pay off the note with highly appreciated assets which will get a step-up in basis on the death of the settlor. The assets within the trust will not get a step-up in basis on the grantor's death, which should be taken into account when evaluating the benefits of a defective grantor trust.

2. Asset Protection Benefits of Defective Grantor Trusts

Although the grantor would be treated as owner of the trust for income tax purposes, he would clearly not have legal or equitable title to the trust's assets. Consequently, trust assets would not be available to the settlor's creditors, unless the trust was treated as a self-settled trust. Because grantors are usually not beneficiaries of defective grantor trusts to avoid inclusion of trust corpus under Code Section 2036, the trust should not be treated as a self-settled trust.

The trust can further be drafted as a spendthrift or a discretionary trust. Further, because the note received from the trust is an interest-only, balloon note, the payment to a creditor of the grantor cannot be accelerated.

Another alternative is to draft the note so that it is personal to the settlor and nonnegotiable. It is possible that making the note nonnegotiable will reduce its value. In that case, the face amount of the note should be increased to ensure that the fair market value of the note equals the value of the property transferred to the trust.

3. Offshore Defective Trusts

An intentionally defective trust with an offshore situs has two advantages.

First, many offshore asset protection jurisdictions have repealed the law against perpetuities, making it possible to set up the trust as a dynasty trust. A dynasty trust can be set up to benefit multiple generations, while being subject to the estate and GST taxes only on the initial funding.

Second, a foreign trust may make it easier to change the trust's status as grantor or non-grantor. In a defective grantor trust, the grantor transfers most of his or her assets to the trust but continues to pay taxes on trust's income. While that is usually very advantageous, it is possible that the grantor will eventually exhaust his or her non-trust assets and will be unable to pay taxes. In that case it may be beneficial to change the trust's status to non-grantor. While that may be accomplished by having the grantor relinquish certain powers, it is even easier to accomplish by changing the trust's classification as foreign or domestic for tax purposes.

If a trust is foreign for tax purposes and has a U. S. beneficiary, it is always a grantor trust. It is relatively simple to reclassify a foreign trust as domestic for tax purposes—simply switching to a U. S. trustee and subjecting the trust to the concurrent jurisdiction of a U.S. court should be sufficient. If the trust is not otherwise drafted as a grantor trust under Code Section 671, it will switch to the non-grantor status.

B. Offshore Trust and Entity Combos

1. Generally

Foreign trusts are most effective when they hold foreign assets. As discussed above, with a stroke of a pen a judge can vest in the creditor any U. S. asset of the debtor, even if the asset is titled in a foreign trust.

However, while that is possible, it does not happen often, and should not happen if the planning is done timely, without concealing any aspects of the plan. Assuming that the trust will not be disregarded by a judge as being separate from the debtor, or simply ignored, what is the best way for the trust to hold U. S. based assets?

For cash and marketable securities, the trust can just hold the assets directly, because they can be moved offshore quickly. The same is not true for real estate or a business operated within the U. S. In that case it is important to ensure that **(i)** the choice of law analysis points offshore, and **(ii)** when the real estate is liquidated, the proceeds go offshore.

The best way to achieve both of those goals is by holding the real estate through a limited liability company organized offshore. This structure has the additional benefits of availing the client of the valuation discounts found in an LLC,[301] and obtaining the additional asset protection by way of the LLC charging order statute of the jurisdiction where the entity is organized.

2. Foreign LLCs

Many foreign jurisdictions have enacted LLC statutes. A lot of these jurisdictions are so-called tax havens, which generally means that an entity organized in that jurisdiction will not be taxed by that jurisdiction if the entity is not conducting any business in the jurisdiction. If a U. S. business or U. S. real estate is owned by an entity organized in a tax haven, the entity will not be doing any business in the tax haven and will not be taxed there.[302]

In most offshore jurisdictions with LLC statutes, the LLC laws are similar to the U. S. state LLC laws. Thus, LLC members enjoy limited liability, and the protection of

---

[301] Obtaining a valuations discount by using an LLC is a complex area of law, based primarily on the Code Section 2036 analysis, and is outside the scope of this outline.

[302] Although the entity will not be "taxed" by the jurisdiction, it will still be subject to annual registration fees.

the charging order. Additionally, many offshore jurisdictions provide that the charging order is the sole remedy of the creditor, with no right to foreclose.

Pursuant to the traditional choice of law analysis, the law of the jurisdiction where an entity is organized will govern the entity, even if the business is transacted elsewhere. For example, California Corporations Code Section 17450(a) provides:

> The laws of the state or foreign country under which a foreign limited liability company is organized shall govern its organization and internal affairs and the ***liability and authority of its managers and members***. [Emphasis added.]

The only time when this choice of law will not be respected is when the application of the laws of the foreign jurisdiction will violate the public policy of the state where the LLC is conducting business. Because the LLC statutes of offshore jurisdictions are very similar to the U. S. LLC statutes, it is unlikely that the offshore statutes will be ignored for public policy reasons.

Thus, as opposed to exporting the assets to a foreign jurisdiction, a foreign LLC allows to import the law. While the asset protection safeguard is not as high, for many debtors it may be the only viable option.

This means that if a California resident organized a Nevis LLC to hold Idaho real estate, a creditor attempting to collect against the California resident would have to rely on the Nevis charging order statute. The Nevis charging order statute limits the creditor to the charging order, with no right to foreclose.[303]

It is important to remember that a foreign entity that does not want to be taxed as a corporation for U. S. tax purposes should make an affirmative election to be taxed as a partnership by filing Form 8832.

Some U. S. jurisdictions (like, Nevada) similarly restrict creditors to the charging order, with no right to foreclose. What is the advantage of a foreign LLC to a domestic LLC all else being equal?

The advantages are: **(i)** extra costs and expenses incurred by a creditor in pursuing a debtor to a foreign jurisdiction, and **(ii)** the favorable asset protection laws of the foreign jurisdiction. Particularly if the jurisdiction, like the Cook Islands, does not recognize U. S. judgments.

3. Combining Foreign Trusts and Foreign LLCs

Combining an LLC and a trust, both organized offshore, has advantages for both entities.

In this structure, the foreign trust is the sole member of an LLC, or, at the very least, the trust holds a super-majority interest in the LLC. This provides further insulation to the assets within the LLC, because now a creditor has to first penetrate the foreign trust, second, obtain a charging order against the LLC and then collect on the charging order. Steps two and three are not easy to accom-

[303] Nevis Limited Liability Company Ordinance Section 43.

plish, but are possible. Step one, penetrating the foreign trust, is possible technically, but not practically.

The use of a foreign LLC also has advantages for debtors planning with foreign trusts. For a debtor to avail itself of the impossibility defense in a contempt situation, the debtor must not have any control over trust assets. However, if the trust owns the LLC, and the debtor is appointed as the LLC's manager, without an ownership interest, the debtor can control the assets, without being in control of the trust.

In the event of threatened litigation the debtor can be either removed as the manager of the LLC, or, preferably, the LLC agreement should give the trust veto power over certain distributions, actions and decisions by the manager. For example, the trust should have veto power over liquidation of the LLC, a distribution exceeding a certain amount, or issuance of a membership interest to a new member.

VIII. Choice of Entity

A. Generally

For someone about to start a new business, one of the first considerations will be the form the business will take. This usually requires a decision as to whether or not to incorporate or pick some other entity form. While tax factors are often the basis for this decision, there are a number of non-tax factors that must be taken into consideration.

Even for existing businesses, alternate entity choices should be considered, provided that the tax burden in converting the entity form is not too great.

In the sole proprietorship, the business is the individual, even though the individual may be conducting the business under a trade name. The sole owner has full authority and responsibility for all business decisions, owns all property as an individual, assumes unlimited liability for all debts of the business, and is taxed as an individual.

The multi-owner business form having the most legal incidents in common with the sole proprietorship is the general partnership. Its two outstanding features are the unlimited liability of each partner for all the debts of the business, and the implied authority of each partner to bind the firm as to outsiders by any act within the scope of the usual and ordinary activities of the particular business.

Between the general partnership and the ordinary business corporation lie a number of organizational forms that have some of the characteristics of both a corporation and a partnership. These include the limited partnership, in which the liability of the limited partners is limited to their investment in the business unless they participate in the "control of the business"; the "joint venture" or "syndicate" which is not readily distinguishable from the general partnership except in that it is ordinarily formed for a single transaction; the joint stock company, in which the ownership is represented by freely transferable shares, there is no general agency on the part of the members to act for the firm, the death or withdrawal of a member does not dissolve the organization, and the shareholders are liable to third persons for debts and tortuous acts of the company except as creditors may otherwise agree; and the business or "Massachusetts" trust, which differs little from the joint-stock company except that management and title to the firm property are vested in trustees who bear personal liability for the trust's debts and its torts.

For most large businesses, especially before the advent of the limited liability company, the corporate form has been the predominant form of entity. Corporations vary widely in the number of shareholders, ranging from:

> **1.** The one-man corporation, in which all the outstanding stock is beneficially owned by one person, and is functionally more closely allied to the sole proprietorship than to the corporation. It may, therefore, be viewed as an "incorporated sole proprietorship."
>
> **2.** The close corporation, in which the stock is held in a few hands, is not publicly traded, and

which is functionally similar to the partnership. It may be viewed as an "incorporated partnership."

3. The public issue corporation, in which share ownership is widely scattered.

All corporations, no matter how many shareholders they have or the amount of their assets, share a number of attributes: **(i)** they are all creatures of statute (no corporation may exist except as the state of its incorporation gives it life and it has no powers other than those granted by statute); **(ii)** they have juristic autonomy (they are legal entities, separate and distinct from their shareholders—they may own property, make contracts, and sue and be sued in their own names); **(iii)** the liability of the shareholders is generally limited to the amount of their investment in the corporation; **(iv)** the life of the corporation is perpetual (It is unaffected by any change in the identity of its shareholders. In the close corporation, however, it is possible for dissident owners to terminate corporate existence through the use of dissolution procedures that are unavailable to holders of minority interests in public issue corporations.); **(v)** there is free transferability of the shareholders' proprietary interests (In the close corporation, however, where the shareholders desire to retain ownership in the hands of a specific group or to prevent share ownership on the part of members of other groups, restrictions on transfer are possible and may be required by the applicable close corporation statute.); and **(vi)** the corporation is managed by or under the control of its board of directors. In a widely-held corporation, management by shareholders is not only undesirable, it would be impossible. But in the close corporation, it is possible to retain management in the shareholder "partners."

The continuity of the existence of a business organization is of great importance to its owners because the "going concern" value of any given enterprise is almost certain to be greater than its value on dissolution. In the case of a sole proprietorship, the business necessarily terminates upon the death of the proprietor; the personal representative may usually carry on the business for the limited period of time necessary to permit its winding up. Potential buyers might be unwilling to purchase the business for fear that key employees would not remain after the death of the owner to whom they had given their personal loyalties. The loss of the sole proprietor's personal services, often a major factor in the going concern value of the business, will often depress its sale value (and its valuation for federal estate tax purposes).

In the case of a general partnership, the usual rule is that the death or withdrawal of one of the partners dissolves the partnership, although an appropriate agreement in the partnership articles, a separate agreement, or the decedent partner's will, may provide for the continuation of the partnership business despite dissolution. In effect, the original partnership is dissolved and a new partnership is created to carry on the enterprise. The new partnership may consist of the former partners plus a new partner who has purchased the partnership interest of the withdrawing or deceased former partner, or the remaining partners may themselves purchase the interest.

The limited partnership is a step closer to the continuously existing organization in part because a limited partner may assign her interest in the venture without effecting dissolution, and the organization is not dissolved by her death. On the other hand, barring a provision to the contrary in the certificate of agreement of all the remaining members, the "death, retirement, or insanity," of a general partner dissolves the firm.

1. Sole Proprietorship

The simplest structure for conducting a business is the individual or sole proprietorship. In this form of business enterprise the individual carries on his business for himself the as sole owner.

With a minimum of legal formalities involved in setting up the business, the sole proprietorship is well suited to the small, one-man business venture. Because the individual retains full ownership, he can operate the business as he chooses with a maximum of flexibility in the use of the business asset. Decision-making and action may be undertaken quickly and easily when no other person is associated with the business.

The basic disadvantages of the sole proprietorship arise from the complete identity of the business entity with the individual doing business. In contrast with the limited-liability characteristic of a corporation or limited partnership, the liabilities of the business venture are the personal liabilities of the individual proprietor. The financial risk of the sole proprietor is not limited to the amount invested in the business but encompasses all of his personal and business assets. This factor is important mainly where the individual possesses extensive assets that are not invested in the business, or where the business conducted is a hazardous or speculative one.

Although the proprietor may utilize the services of others by hiring them as servants or agents, his business will be unable to expand beyond his own acumen and practical abilities. Thus, other forms of conducting business may be necessary when the scope of the business requires more and varied specialized business talent than the sole proprietor alone can supply.

A further consequence which flows from the complete identity of the business entity with the proprietor himself, is the termination of the business as a legal unit upon his death. Although the owner may take steps designed to continue the business after his death, there is no assurance of continuity of existence. It is important that the sole proprietor make provision for the problems which arise at death, from the standpoint of sound estate planning as well as other business considerations. Statutory provision for continuity of existence of certain businesses after death is present in some jurisdictions.

Note: For a sole proprietor, incorporating the business may prove of limited significance from an asset protection standpoint. Consider the case of a baby sitter who decides to incorporate her business. The baby sitter forms a corporation and the corporation contracts with the baby's parents to provide baby-sitting services. While only the corporation and not the baby sitter personally will be liable for contract claims, the same is not true of tort claims. If the baby sitter commits an act of tort, the baby's parents will be able to sue, not only the corporation, but also the person who committed the tort—the baby sitter.

2. General Partnership

The general partnership is an association of two or more persons carrying on a business enterprise for a profit. Under California law, a general partnership may be formed even if there is no intent to form a partnership.[304] A general partnership is an entity distinct from its partners, and can thus own property and conduct business under its own name. Each partner is an agent of the partnership for the purpose of its business, and the act of any partner for apparently carrying on in the usual way the business of the partnership binds the partnership unless the partner actually lacks authority to do so and the other party has knowledge of that fact.

Partners are jointly and severally liable for most wrongdoings for which the partnership is liable and jointly liable for all other debts and obligations of the partnership.

Unless specifically otherwise agreed among partners, no one can become a partner of a partnership without the consent of all of the partners

A partnership is dissolved, among other things, by the dissociation of any partner unless a majority in interest of the partners (including rightfully dissociating partners) agree to continue the partnership, and by a number of other specific events.[305]

---

[304] California Corp. Code Section 16202(a).
[305] California Corp. Code Section 16801(2)(A).

3. Limited Liability Partnership

Those professionals engaged in the practice of architecture, law or public accountancy can form an entity known as a limited liability partnership ("LLP").[306] Each partner in an LLP can participate in the management and control of the entity, similar to partners in a general partnership.

An LLP partner is not liable for the debts and obligations of the LLP or tortious conduct of other partners if the LLP is registered as an LLP, has a certificate of registration from the California State Bar if it is a law LLP, and if the security requirements are satisfied.[307] Partners in LLPs may be personally liable under certain circumstances for their own acts. In particular, a partner of an LLP is liable for personal tortious conduct (including malpractice claims against the partner).[308]

4. Limited Partnership

A limited partnership is a partnership that has one or more general partners, and also one or more limited partners.[309] The more important attributes of a limited partnership that differ from those of a general partnership are:

> **1.** A limited partner normally is not liable for obligations of the partnership beyond the amount of his, her, or its capital contributed or agreed to be

---

[306] California Corp. Code Section 16101(4)(A), (B).
[307] California Corp. Code Sections 16306(c), 16956.
[308] California Corp. Code Section 16306(e).
[309] California Corp. Code Sections 15509, 15643(b).

contributed;[310] a general partner in a limited partnership is personally liable for all of its obligations.[311]

2. A limited partner may not participate in the control of the business (except for the exercise of certain rights and powers of a limited partner expressly excluded from acts constituting "control")[312] without losing limited status and becoming liable as a general partner.

3. A limited partnership interest is assignable, but the assignment does not dissolve the partnership or entitle the assignee to become or to exercise the rights of a partner. The assignment only entitles the assignee to receive, to the extent assigned, the distributions and the allocations of income, gain, loss, deduction, credit, or similar item to which the assignor would be entitled.[313]

5. Corporation

The corporation is a creature of state statute and may only be formed by registering it with the state (in California, the Secretary of State). The costs to form a corporation are relatively modest, and the formation process is simple.

The corporation is one of the oldest forms of entity, and has been used for centuries to pool investments from many

---

[310] California Corp. Code Section 15632(a).
[311] California Corp. Code Sections 15509, 15643(b).
[312] California Corp. Code Section 15632(b).
[313] California Corp. Code Section 15672(a).

different investors to conduct a common business. Corporations have several defining characteristics, such as an unlimited life, centralized management, and limited liability of shareholders.

Corporate shareholders have been traditionally given limited liability to foster investments and growth of business enterprises. The liability of shareholders is limited to their investment in the corporation. This means that any other assets that the shareholder may own will not be held liable for any corporate liabilities. The only asset that the shareholder stands to lose is his or her investment in the corporation. This rule holds true even for one shareholder corporations.

One of the exceptions to the limited liability of shareholders is the **alter ego doctrine**, also known as piercing the corporate veil. The doctrine stands for the proposition that while corporations are treated as separate entities under state law, that will remain true only if the shareholders treat the corporation as a separate entity. Where the shareholders most commonly run afoul of the alter ego doctrine is in commingling funds and not maintaining corporate formalities. Additionally, alter ego arguments can be based on lack of capitalization of the corporation on formation.

Commingling occurs when assets are combined in a common fund or account. In order to prevent commingling, the corporation and its shareholders should maintain separate accounts. Any loans that are made between the shareholder and the corporation should be clearly documented by notes. Where commingling is present, it is difficult to distinguish between the corporation and the individual. Consequently, the two are treated as one.

Corporations, being a creature of statute, have to comply with numerous statutory and regulatory requirements. One of the requirements is that corporations have to maintain certain corporate formalities, including keeping separate corporate records, holding annual meetings and keeping minutes of meetings, issuing stock, electing directors and officers, and avoiding commingling of funds.

There has been a recent movement to modernize the corporate formalities law. For example, California has significantly decreased the amount of formalities that closely-held corporations have to comply with. Specifically, California Corporations Code Section 300(e) eliminates most normal formalities of corporate operation through provisions in a shareholders' agreement waiving such formalities. Thus, Section 300(e) explicitly provides that the failure of a close corporation to observe corporate formalities relating to meetings of directors or shareholders in connection with the management of its affairs, pursuant to a shareholders' agreement, shall not be considered a factor tending to establish that the shareholders have personal liability for corporate obligations.

It is very important to remember that piercing the corporate veil can work in either direction. Most commonly, the veil is pierced when the creditor attempts to go from the corporation to the shareholders. Reverse piercing is also possible when the shareholder is sued, and the creditor attempts to disregard the corporate existence and proceeds after the corporate assets. In reverse piercing cases, similar factors and tests are considered by the courts.

In addition to the alter ego doctrine, one should remember that there are other ways that corporate shareholders may get exposed to personal liability, such as guaranteeing the corporate debt, being personally liable for certain types of corporate liabilities due to a specific statute (such as Superfund clean-up costs, and trust fund taxes), and acting as a shareholder and as a director or officer.

6. Limited Liability Company

The limited liability company ("LLC"), a relatively recent creature of state statute, is a non-corporate entity that combines the flexibility of a partnership with limited liability for all of its members, even if they participate actively in its management. An LLC can be structured so that it is not subject to federal income tax at the entity level, but receives the pass-through treatment applied to a partnership. Alternatively, when state law allows (as does California), the organizers may, in certain cases, prefer to create an LLC that is taxable as a corporation.

An LLC differs from a limited partnership in that all of the members of an LLC can participate actively in the management of the firm without becoming personally liable to third parties for its obligations. And it differs from a Subchapter S corporation in that there is no maximum number of owners that an LLC may have and its members can be either natural persons or other entities and have different types of interests. Thus, the LLC has emerged primarily as a small-business alternative to the limited partnership and the Subchapter S corporation. In some states, LLCs can be established by practitioners of professions for rendering professional services. California is not one of these states.

An LLC is formed by filing its articles of organization (Form LLC-1) with the Secretary of State. The state statutes generally grant LLC members much flexibility in determining how their business will be run; many statutory provisions operate only by default, when the members fail to provide differently by agreement. Most of the rules governing the internal operations of an LLC are contained in the members' private operating agreement, comparable to a partnership agreement or corporate by-laws.

Unless the operating agreement provides otherwise, management of an LLC is usually vested by statute in its members. However, members may choose to delegate their management authority to a particular member or group of members, or, in some cases, to a non-member manager. LLC members typically vote and share in profits, losses and distributions in proportion to the value of their contributions.

Under many LLC statutes, fundamental changes within the business require the unanimous approval of the members. Thus, all members must consent to the admission of new members; without such consent, assignees of LLC interests may not participate in management, although they may receive the income earned by their interests. Upon any member's death, retirement, resignation, expulsion, bankruptcy, or dissolution, the LLC is usually dissolved unless the remaining members agree to continue the entity. However, the members may change the unanimous consent requirement by agreement.

A membership interest in an LLC is personal property. Real and personal property transferred to or acquired by an LLC is property of the entity rather than the members individually, and property may be conveyed in the LLC's name. These provisions establish a more definite system of property ownership than exists under partnership law.

LLC members receive the same liability protection as corporate shareholders for the liabilities of the entity.[314] Further, similar to corporations and limited partnerships, the LLC does not shield its members from their own torts or failure to comply with tax withholding obligations.

LLC members are subject to the same alter ego piercing theories as corporate shareholders.[315] However, it is more difficult to pierce the LLC veil because LLCs do not have a great many formalities to maintain. So long as the LLC and the members do not commingle funds, it would be difficult to pierce its veil.

B. Charging Order Protection

1. Protecting Assets within Entities

Often, asset protection practitioners will talk about inside out and outside in asset protection. This is a critical distinction.

Example: Dr. Brown is a neurosurgeon. He owns two apartment buildings having a combined equity of $10 million. Apartment building "A" is owned by Dr. Brown through a corporation, while apartment building "B" is owned through a limited liability company, taxed as a partnership for income tax purposes.

---

[314] California Corp. Code Section 17101(a).
[315] California Corp. Code Section 17101(b).

Assume that two tenants, one residing in a building A and the other in building B, slip, fall and sue, and Dr. Brown's general liability insurance policy is insufficient to cover the claims. Because the buildings are owned by a corporation and a limited liability company, the tenants have to sue these two entities. If the tenants are successful, they will be able to recover against the entities, but, ordinarily, will not be able to pierce the entities and go after the individual owners, namely, Dr. Brown.

Assume now that two of Dr. Brown's patients sue Dr. Brown and the judgment exceeds the limits of Dr. Brown's malpractice policy. The patients will attempt to enforce the judgment against all of Dr. Brown's assets, including his interests in the corporation and the LLC.

The patient-creditor will be able to obtain a writ of execution or a turnover order against Dr. Brown's interest in the corporation, effectively getting apartment building A.

This is an extremely important point to remember. Corporations are often thought of as limited liability entities. The referenced limited liability is that of the shareholder when the corporation is sued. The same limited liability does not apply to the corporation when the shareholder is sued.

2. Charging Order Limitation

Returning to Dr. Brown, what happens to apartment building B, the one owned by the LLC? Fortunately for Dr. Brown, the result is different.

Membership interests in LLCs and partnership interests are afforded a significant level of protection through the charging order mechanism. The charging order limits the creditor of a debtor-partner or a debtor-member to the debtor's share of distributions, without conferring on the creditor any voting or management rights. While that may not seem like much at first glance, in practice, the charging order limitation is a very powerful asset protection tool.

a. The Importance of History

Before the advent of the charging order,[316] a creditor pursuing a partner in a partnership was able to obtain from the court a writ of execution directly against the partnership's assets, which led to the seizure of such assets by the sheriff. This result was possible because the partnership itself was not treated as a juridical person, but simply as an aggregate of its partners.

The seizure of partnership assets was usually carried out by the sheriff, who would go down to the partnership's place of business and shut it down. That caused the non-debtor partners to suffer financial losses, sometimes on par with the debtor partner, and the process was considered to be entirely "clumsy."[317]

To protect the non-debtor partners from the creditor of the debtor-partner it was necessary to keep the creditor from seizing partnership assets (which was also in line with

---

[316] The first charging order statute appeared in Section 23 of the English Partnership Act of 1890, and was later picked up by the Uniform Partnership Act (Section 28) of 1914, and the Uniform Limited Partnership Act (Section 22) of 1916.
[317] Brown, Janson & Co. v. A. Hutchinson & Co., 1895 Q.B. 737 (Eng. C.A.).

the developing perception of partnerships as legal entities and not simple aggregates of partners) and to keep the creditor out of partnership affairs. These objectives could only be accomplished by limiting the collection remedies that creditors previously enjoyed. Because any limitation on a creditor's remedies is a boon to the debtor, over the years charging orders have come to be perceived as asset protection devices.

The rationale behind the charging order applied initially only to general partnerships, where every partner was involved in carrying on the business of the partnership; it did not apply to corporations because of their centralized management structure.[318] However, over the years the charging order protection was extended to limited partners and LLC members.

b. The Uniform Acts

Both partnership statutes and limited liability company statutes (in most domestic and foreign jurisdictions that have these entity types) provide for charging orders. In almost all the states (including California) partnership and LLC statutes are based on the uniform acts, such as the Revised Uniform Partnership Act of 1994 ("RUPA"), the Uniform Limited Partnership Act of 2001 ("ULPA") or the

---

[318] Because charging orders do not apply to corporations, a creditor of a shareholder can attach the shares of corporate stock owned by the debtor-shareholder and obtain the entire bundle of rights inherent in those shares, including liquidation and voting rights.

Uniform Limited Liability Company Act of 1996 ("ULLCA"), or the earlier versions of these acts.

The very first references to the charging order (in the United States) appeared in Section 28 of the Uniform Partnership Act of 1914 and Section 22 of the Uniform Limited Partnership Act of 1916 and allowed creditors to petition the court for a charging order against the debtor's partnership interest. Both statutes, directly or indirectly, addressed the fact that the charging order was not the exclusive remedy of the creditor. Appointment of a receiver and foreclosure of the partnership interest were anticipated.

The subsequent amendment to the Uniform Limited Partnership Act (in 1976), clarified the charging order remedy by stating that the judgment creditor had the rights of an assignee of the partnership interest.

The RUPA, at Section 504, and the ULLCA, at Section 504, introduced the following new concepts: **(i)** the charging order constitutes a lien on the judgment debtor's transferable interest; **(ii)** the purchaser at a foreclosure sale has the rights of a transferee; and **(iii)** the charging order is the exclusive means by which the creditor could pursue the partnership interest.

Both acts also provide that the charging order does not charge the entire partnership or membership interest of the debtor, but only the "transferable" (RUPA) or "distributional" (ULLCA) interest. However, the language providing that the creditor has the rights of an assignee was dropped.

The ULPA (the last act, chronologically), in addition to the new language in the RUPA and the ULLCA provides, further, at Section 703, that **(i)** the judgment creditor has only the rights of a transferee,[319] and **(ii)** the court may order a foreclosure only on the transferable interest.[320]

All three most recent acts also provide that the charged interest may be redeemed prior to foreclosure.[321]

There are four important points to take away from the wording of these uniform acts: **(1)** the charging order is a lien on the judgment debtor's transferable/distributional interest, it is not a levy, **(2)** the creditor can never exercise any management or voting rights because the creditor has only the rights of an assignee/transferee, **(3)** the foreclosure of the charged interest does not harm the debtor because the buyer at the foreclosure sale receives no greater right than was possessed by the original creditor, and **(4)** the creditor, expressly, has no other remedies, but the charging order (and foreclosure on the charging order).

Because the charging order creates a lien and not a levy, and because the creditor is not even a transferee under ULPA, but only has the rights of a transferee, the creditor does not become the owner of the charged interest unless there is foreclosure. This has important tax ramifications (which are discussed below).

By calling the creditor an assignee/transferee, or by stating that the creditor has the rights of an assignee/transferee, the uniform acts deprive the creditor of any voting, man-

---

[319] ULPA, Section 703(a).
[320] ULPA, Section 703(b).
[321] RUPA Section 504(c), ULLCA Section 504(c), ULPA Section 703(c).

agement or access to information rights.[322] Let us use ULPA to see how that happens.

ULPA defines a "transferable interest" as a right to receive distributions.[323] A "transferee" is defined as a person who receives a transferable interest.[324] ULPA defines two bundles of rights that a partner may have in a partnership: economic rights and other rights.[325] While economic rights are freely transferable, other rights (which include management and voting rights) are not transferable at all, unless provided otherwise in the partnership agreement.[326]

ULPA further clarifies that a transferee only has the right to receive distributions, if and when made.[327] This is further elaborated upon by comments to the charging order section of ULPA:

> This section balances the needs of a judgment creditor of a partner or transferee with the needs of the limited partnership and non-debtor partners and transferees. The section achieves that balance by allowing the judgment creditor to collect on the judgment through the transferable interest of the judgment debtor while prohibiting interference in

---

[322] This is a reflection of two principles: (i) the creditor should be kept out of the entity so that the non-debtor owners are not inconvenienced, and (ii) the so-called "pick your partner" philosophy that allows partners and members to approve any new incoming partner/member. See, for example, RUPA, Section 401(i).
[323] ULPA Section 102(22).
[324] ULPA Section 102(23).
[325] ULPA Section 701.
[326] *Id.*
[327] *Id.*

> the management and activities of the limited partnership.
>
> Under this section, the judgment creditor of a partner or transferee is entitled to a charging order against the relevant transferable interest. While in effect, that order entitles the judgment creditor to whatever distributions would otherwise be due to the partner or transferee whose interest is subject to the order. The creditor has no say in the timing or amount of those distributions. The charging order does not entitle the creditor to accelerate any distributions or to otherwise interfere with the management and activities of the limited partnership.
>
> Foreclosure of a charging order effects a permanent transfer of the charged transferable interest to the purchaser. The foreclosure does not, however, create any rights to participate in the management and conduct of the limited partnership's activities. The purchaser obtains nothing more than the status of a transferee.[328]

ULLCA has similar provisions that restrict the creditor to a "distributional interest" (identical, except in name, to ULPA "transferable interest") that does not confer on the creditor any voting or management rights.[329]

The creditor's inability to vote the charged interest or participate in the management of the entity is at the heart of the asset protection efficacy of the charging order. If the

---

[328] ULPA Section 703, Comments.
[329] ULLCA Sections 101(6), 501-504.

partnership or the LLC halts all distributions, the creditor has no ability to force the distributions.

Much fear has been expressed by some practitioners about the creditor's ability to foreclose.[330] This fear appears to be entirely unfounded—the uniform acts clearly provide that only the charged interest may be foreclosed upon, and further provide that the purchaser at the foreclosure sale has only the rights of a transferee. To grant the purchaser of the foreclosed interest an interest greater than the right to receive distributions would mean granting to the purchaser voting and management rights associated with the debtor's interest in the entity. That would be contrary to the very reason why charging order statutes exist in the first place.

A creditor holding a charging order usually does not know whether any distributions will be forthcoming from the entity. This uncertainty is of little value to most creditors. But it may be possible to find a third party, possibly a collection firm, that may buy the charged interest at a steep discount and then wait to get paid (which may be folly due to possible adverse tax consequences). Consequently, the ability to foreclose affords the creditor some limited value.

The creditor's ability to foreclose is not, in any way, detrimental to the debtor. So long as no one can take away the debtor's management and voting rights, the debtor is not made worse off.

---

[330] See, for example, Elizabeth M. Schurig and Amy P. Jetel, *A Charging Order is the Exclusive Remedy Against a Partnership Interest: Fact or Fiction?,* Prob. & Prop. (Nov./Dec. 2003). See also the critique of the above referenced article in the same publication: Daniel S. Kleinberger, Carter G. Bishop and Thomas Earl Geu, *Charging Orders and the New Uniform Limited Partnership Act: Dispelling Rumors of Disaster*, Prob. & Prop. (Jul./Aug. 2004).

The exclusivity of the charging order (including the ability to foreclose on the charging order), which may be found in each recent uniform act, relates back to the origin of the charging order. The drafters of the uniform acts did not want to allow the creditor any possibility of gaining voting or management rights, and the exclusivity language should be read in that light.

A common point of confusion needs to be addressed with respect to exclusivity. Many cases dealing with charging orders focus on whether the charging order is the exclusive creditor remedy, or whether foreclosure is authorized (see discussion below). The uniform acts, until RUPA in 1994, never made the charging order the exclusive creditor remedy, although it was always understood that the creditor can never gain management rights. Beginning with RUPA, all uniforms acts have introduced the element of exclusivity, but it is not the charging order that is made the exclusive remedy. Instead, the acts make the respective sections of the acts dealing with charging orders the exclusive remedy, and these sections specifically allow foreclosure.

Some practitioners and commentators[331] have suggested that the exclusivity language may mean that fraudulent transfer laws would not apply to transfers of assets to partnerships or limited liability companies.[332] While a strict reading of the exclusivity language may, at first glance, suggest such an outcome, it would be incorrect. The charging order limitation protects the debtor's interest in the le-

---

[331] See the discussion of the Alaska charging order statute in the Kleinberger, Bishop and Geu article.
[332] Find cite, was mentioned in one of the articles

gal entity. If a creditor successfully establishes that a transfer of assets to a legal entity is a fraudulent transfer (which would be a separate legal action from the application for a charging order), the creditor no longer needs to pursue the debtor's interest in the entity. With a fraudulent transfer judgment, the creditor gains the ability to pursue the entity itself, in its capacity as the transferee of the assets. Accordingly, if the creditor has the ability to pursue the partnership or the LLC, the protection of the debtor's interest in the entity through the charging order becomes a moot point. Several courts have now opined on this subject as well, uniformly holdings that the exclusivity language of the charging order statutes is not a bar to a fraudulent transfer challenge.[333]

c. California Statutes on Charging Orders

CCP Section 708.310 provides:

> If a money judgment is rendered against a partner but not against the partnership, the judgment debtor's interest in the partnership may be applied toward the satisfaction of the judgment by an order charging the judgment debtor's interest pursuant to Section 15029 or 15673 of the Corporations Code.

---

[333] See, for example, Taylor v. S & M Lamp Co., 190 Cal. App. 2d 700, 708 (1961); Chrysler Credit Corp. v. Peterson, 342 N.W. 2d 170, 172 (Minn. 1984); Firmani v. Firmani, 332 N.J. Super. 118, 752 A.2d 854 (N.J. 2000).

In turn, Section 15673 of the Corporations Code provides:

> On application to a court of competent jurisdiction by any judgment creditor of a partner, the court may charge the limited partnership interest of the partner with payment of the unsatisfied amount of the judgment with interest. To the extent so charged, the judgment creditor has only the rights of an assignee of the limited partnership interest.

Section 15672 then provides:

> An assignment of a limited partnership interest does not dissolve a limited partnership or, other than as set forth in this chapter, entitle the assignee to become or to exercise any rights of a partner. An assignment entitles the assignee to receive, to the extent assigned, the distributions and the allocations of income, gain, loss, deduction, credit, or similar item, to which the assignor would be entitled.

Section 17302(a) of the Corporations Code provides similarly with respect to limited liability companies:

> On application by a judgment creditor of a member or of a member's assignee, a court having jurisdiction may charge the assignable membership interest of the judgment debtor to satisfy the judgment.

Section 17301 then provides:

> (a)(1) A membership interest or an economic interest is assignable in whole or in part, provided, however, that no membership interest may be assigned without the consent of a majority in interest of the members not transferring their interests.
>
> (a)(2) An assignment of an economic interest does not of itself dissolve the limited liability company or, other than as set forth in the articles of organization or operating agreement, entitle the assignee to vote or participate in the management and affairs of the limited liability company or to become or exercise any rights of a member.
>
> (a)(3) An assignment of an economic interest merely entitles the assignee to receive, to the extent assigned, the distributions and the allocations of income, gains, losses, deductions, credit, or similar items to which the assignor would be entitled.

The "membership interest" is defined in Section 17001(z) as:

> Membership interest means a member's rights in the limited liability company, collectively, including the member's economic interest, any right to vote or participate in management, and any right to

information concerning the business and affairs of the limited liability company provided by this title.

The "economic interest" is defined in Section 17001(n) as:

> Economic interest means a person's right to share in the income, gains, losses, deductions, credit, or similar items of, and to receive distributions from, the limited liability company, but does not include any other rights of a member, including, without limitation, the right to vote or to participate in management, or, except as provided in Section 17106, any right to information concerning the business and affairs of the limited liability company.

Similar rules apply to general partnerships.[334]

These statutes bring up an interesting question that should be considered by anyone seeking asset protection. If the charging order confers on the creditor assignable/transferable interests, or the rights of an assignee/transferee, can those rights be further restricted?

All uniform acts and state statutes define these terms, and in some way limit assignable/transferable interests to various economic rights, *i.e.*, the right to receive distributions of cash and property. However, all statutes also allow partners and members to enter into agreements—

---

[334] Corp. Code Section 16504(a).

partnership agreements, limited partnership agreements and operating agreements—and to define various rights and interests in those agreements. What would happen if an operating agreement provided that **(i)** no interests in the LLC may be assigned under any circumstances (not even an economic interest), **(ii)** no interests may be assigned without the consent of the other members/partners, or the consent of the manager or the general partner, or **(iii)** interests may not be assigned to a creditor?

ULLCA specifically provides that members may enter into an operating agreement which would define their respective rights and relationships, and enumerates which statutory provisions the members may not waive through the operating agreement.[335] The comment to Section 103 confirms that in the operating agreement the members may override any provision of ULLCA, other than those specifically listed in Section 103.

> This section makes clear that the only matters an operating agreement may not control are specified in subsection (b). Accordingly, an operating agreement may modify or eliminate any rule specified in any section of this Act except matters specified in subsection (b). To the extent not otherwise mentioned in subsection (b), every section of this Act is simply a default rule, regardless of whether the lan-

---

[335] ULLCA Section 103.

guage of the section appears to be otherwise mandatory.[336]

ULLCA provides, further, that as far as the managers, members and transferees are concerned, the operating agreement is more powerful than the articles of organization.[337]

The same line of reasoning may be found in the other uniform acts and the related state statutes.[338]

To date, only a couple of courts have considered this issue as it relates to charging orders. In California, an appellate court gave due consideration to the terms of the partnership agreement in determining whether a creditor could foreclose on a partnership interest.[339] In a Nevada Supreme Court opinion, the court stated that "the partnership agreements could not divest the district court of its powers provided by statute to charge and sell an interest of a partner in a partnership."[340] However, this statement by the Nevada court is a logical fallacy, as it presumes that the statute gives the court the power to sell the partnership interest. The statute can be interpreted, as described above, to grant

---

[336] ULLCA Section 103, Comment. See also, ULLCA Section 110, Reporters' Notes ("A limited liability company is as much a creature of contract as of statute, and the operating agreement is the 'cornerstone' of the typical LLC."
[337] ULLCA Section 203(c).
[338] See, for example, ULPA Section 110; Corp. Code Section 17301(a) (this section discusses the assignability of membership interests, unless provided otherwise in the operating agreement); Colorado Revised Statutes Section 7-80-108.
[339] Crocker Nat. Bank v. Perroton, 208 Cal. App. 3d 1, 255 Cal. Rptr. 794 (1989).
[340] Tupper v. Kroc, 88 Nev. 146, 154 (1972).

the court the ability to sell the partnership interest only when it is allowed by the partnership agreement.

If asset protection is the primarily or sole reason for setting up the limited partnership or the LLC, the partner/member may have nothing to lose by adding, in some form, the non-assignability language. The author particularly favors granting a third-party manager approval rights over assignability and transferability of all interests, including economic rights. The downside of this practice would cause one to default to the standard charging order rules discussed above. The upside would deprive the creditor even from the right to receive distributions. This strategy will not work in Delaware, because the creditor is expressly granted the right to receive distributions.

d. Charging Order Cases

There are not a great many cases on charging orders, primarily for two reasons. First, many creditors fail to find the charging order to be a useful remedy, and seek to settle with the debtor rather than hoping to get a distribution out of the entity. Second, even when creditors pursue the charging order remedy, the charging order is granted by a trial court and is rarely appealed, so there are few published opinions. Many of the reported cases deal with the creditor's ability to foreclose; most cases authorize the creditor to foreclose but restrict the buyer of the interest to the economic component of the interest. There are also some interesting outliers, readily demonstrating the degree of judicial imagination involved in statutory interpretation.

The California Supreme Court has affirmed that the charging order has replaced levies of execution as the remedy for reaching partnership interests.[341] The two most interesting charging order cases out of California are Crocker Nat. Bank v. Perroton,[342] and Hellman v. Anderson.[343]

In Crocker, the court concluded that a partnership interest may be foreclosed upon if the sale of the interest does not violate the partnership agreement and the other partners consent to the sale.[344] In Hellman, the court confirmed that foreclosure of the charged interest is authorized by the charging order statute, but disagreed with Crocker that consent of non-debtor partners is required. The court concluded that consent from other partners is not required because pursuant to the foreclosure sale, the buyer receives only the economic interest in the partnership, but not voting or management rights. Consequently, the buyer will never have ability to interfere with the business of the partnership and inconvenience the non-debtor partners.[345] Going even further, the Hellman court remanded the case back to trial court for a determination whether the foreclosure of the economic interest (limited as that interest may be) would unduly interfere with the partnership business.[346]

---

[341] Baum v. Baum, 51 Cal. 2d 610, 612, 335 P. 2d 481, 483 (1959).
[342] 208 Cal. App. 3d 1, 255 Cal. Rptr. 794 (1989).
[343] 233 Cal. App. 3d 840, 284 Cal. Rptr. 830 (1991).
[344] Crocker at 9.
[345] Hellman at 852.
[346] *Id.* at 853.

In the only reported Florida opinion,[347] the court concluded that the simplicity of the language of the charging order statute—"the judgment creditor has only the rights of an assignee"—"necessarily" precluded foreclosure.[348] Florida statutes were subsequently amended to specifically preclude foreclosure (see above).

A Minnesota court held that the "exclusivity" of the charging order must be read in conjunction with the Uniform Fraudulent Conveyances Act.[349] In this case a limited partnership interest subject to a charging order was transferred in a fraudulent conveyance to the debtor's wife and attorney. The creditor was allowed to pursue the limited partnership interest transferred through the fraudulent conveyance and retain its charging order.

In Deutsch v. Wolff,[350] a Missouri court analyzed, in a charging order context, the receiver's right to manage the partnership. The court drew a distinction between a creditor who becomes an assignee of the debtor-partner (no management rights), and a receiver appointed by the court. A receiver may be granted management rights "when manager of a partnership has willfully engaged in a series of illegal activities…"[351] It seems that in this case the court found the ability to appoint the receiver through the Missouri charging order statute, but vested the receiver with management rights using equity arguments unrelated to the

---

[347] A prior decision in Myrick v. Second National Bank of Clearwater, 335 So. 2d 343 (1976) was made under Florida's version of UPA and has been superseded by the subsequent adoption of RUPA.
[348] Givens v. National Loan Investors L.P., 724 So. 2d 610 (1998).
[349] Chrysler Credit Corp. at 172-173.
[350] 7 S.W. 3d 460 (1999).
[351] *Id.* at 464.

charging order (*i.e.*, a receiver could have been appointed simply because the general partner was defrauding the limited partners). A similar conclusion, under similar circumstances, was reached by courts in Nevada,[352] Kansas[353] and Minnesota.[354]

In Baker v. Dorfman,[355] a New York district court assigned 75% of the single-member's interest in an LLC (the assignment was limited to the profits of the LLC) to the judgment creditor (pursuant to the New York LLC charging order statutes) and appointed a receiver. The receiver was empowered by a magistrate not only to collect the profits, but also to participate in the management of the LLC and to work to increase its profitability. The LLC itself was also a debtor of the judgment creditor in its capacity as a successor in liability of the member-debtor.

The magistrate's ability to do anything but collect profits was later affirmed (with minor modifications) by the Second Circuit.[356] By granting the receiver the ability to manage the LLC, the court certainly went far beyond New York's charging order statute (discussed above). Similar to Deutsch, Tupper, Arkansas City and Windom, there were allegations of fraud against the debtor, and appointment of the receiver may have been possible even absent a charging order. These cases seem to reaffirm that a debtor subject to

---

[352] Tupper at 155.
[353] Arkansas City v. Anderson, 242 Kan. 875, 752 P. 2d 673 (Kan. 1988).
[354] Windom Nat'l Bank v. Klein, 254 N.W. 602, 605 (Minn. 1934).
[355] 2000 U.S. Dist. LEXIS 10142 (S.D.N.Y. 2000), affirmed in part and reversed in part in 232 F.3d 121 (2000).
[356] 232 F. 3d 121, 122 (2000).

a charging order cannot lose its management rights because of the charging order.

In a different New York decision, the court concluded that the charging order was not the sole remedy authorized by the charging order statute, and that levy of the charged interest was proper.[357] The court did make it apparent that the levy did not confer on the creditor a greater interest than the one obtained through the charging order.

e. Single-Member LLCs

Single-member LLCs deserve special attention in the charging order analysis. It may be argued that given the historical framework of charging orders, their protection should not extend to single member LLCs (there are no other "partners" to protect from the creditor).

However, neither the uniform acts nor any of the state charging order statutes makes any distinction between single-member and multi-member LLCs. Some courts have held that the charging order protection would apply in a case where all of the partners of a limited partnership were the debtors of a single creditor.[358] The creditor had argued to no avail that because there were no "innocent" (non-debtor) partners to protect, the charging order protection should not apply.

---

[357] Princeton Bank and Trust Company v. Berley, 57 A.D. 2d 348, 394 N.Y.S. 2d 714 (1977). See, also, *Beckley v. Speaks*, 240 N.Y.S. 2d 553 (1963).

[358] Evans v. Galardi , 16 Cal. 3d 300 (Cal. 1976).

One bankruptcy court held that the charging order protection does not apply to single-member LLCs.[359] In Albright, the debtor was the sole member and manager of an LLC. The bankruptcy trustee asserted that it acquired the right to control the LLC and sell its assets, while the debtor sought to deny those rights to the trustee, based on the above discussion of charging orders.

The bankruptcy court concluded that based on the Colorado LLC statutes, a membership interest in an LLC can be assigned, including management rights.[360] The relevant statute provides that if all the other members do not approve of the assignment, then the assignee does not acquire management rights.[361] If all the other members do approve, then the assignee may become a substituted member (and acquire all rights of a member).[362]

Because in a single-member LLC there are no other members that can "not approve," an assignee will always become a substituted member. The statute was obviously never revised following the introduction of single-member LLCs. The bankruptcy court concluded that if the LLC in Albright was a multi-member LLC, a different result would be reached and the bankruptcy trustee would be entitled only to the distributions of profits, but not management and control over the LLC.[363]

The court's application of the Colorado assignability statutes is faulty. These statutes are implicated only when a

---

[359] In re Albright, 291 B. R. 538 (Bankr. D. Colo. 2003).
[360] Colo. Rev. Stat. Section 7-80-702.
[361] Colo. Rev. Stat. Section 7-80-702(1).
[362] Colo. Rev. Stat. Section 7-80-702(2).
[363] Albright at 541.

member dies or assigns its interest, not in the context of bankruptcy.[364]

The Albright case is often interpreted as a case on single-member LLC charging orders. However, the bankruptcy court devoted most of its analysis to the assignability of interests statutes, and only in passing noted that the debtor made a charging order argument. The court dismissed the debtor's charging order argument out of hand, noting that charging orders were intended to protect non-debtor "partners," and in single-member LLCs there is no one to protect.[365]

The very limited analysis of charging orders engaged in by the Albright court is troubling. The court analyzes and follows Colorado statutes when dealing with the assignability of interests and determining how the charging order would work in a multi-member context. For an unexplained reason, the court completely abandons the Colorado statutes in determining the applicability of the charging order. The Colorado charging order statute does not exempt single-member LLCs from the protection of the charging order.[366] The court completely ignores that and focuses on the historical framework of charging orders.

When there is a clear statute on point, engaging in the analysis of legislative intent and historical origins of statutes is inappropriate.[367] The Colorado charging order stat-

---

[364] Colo. Rev. Stat. Sections 7-80-702 and 7-80-704.
[365] *Id.* at 542-543.
[366] Colorado Revised Statutes Section 7-80-703.
[367] See, e.g., Robert E. v. Justice Court, 99 Nev. 443, 445, 664 P.2d 957, 959 (1983) ("When presented with a question of statutory interpretation, the intent of the legislature is the controlling factor and, if the

ute clearly limits the creditor to an economic interest in the LLC.[368] When the Colorado legislature introduced the single-member LLC statute it is presumed to have known of the charging order statute.[369] It chose not to make any changes to the latter. The Albright decision conveniently ignores these legal principles.[370]

In Albright, the court concluded that if the analysis was carried out under the Colorado charging order statute, and there was another member with a passive interest of an "infinitesimal" nature, the bankruptcy trustee would not acquire any management or control rights.[371]

In Olmstead, 2010 WL 2518106 (July 6, 2010), the debtor was the member of a Florida LLC, which, like California, permits single-member LLC's. The creditor—the FTC—sought to obtain an order permitting the attachment and sale of the debtor's membership interest, similar to the attachment of a share of corporate stock. Florida has a charging order statute similar to California's. The key provision in the Florida charging order statute provides that an

---

statute under consideration is clear on its face, a court can not go beyond the statute in determining legislative intent.")

[368] *Id.*

[369] See, *e.g.*, Sutherland, *Statutory Interpretation*, Section 22.33 (C. Sands 4th ed. 1972); Walen v. Department of Corrections, 443 Mich. 240, 248, 505 N.W.2d 519, 522 (1993); McLeod v. Santa Fe Trail Transp. Co., 205 Ark. 225, 230, 168 S.W.2d 413, 416 (1943); Woodson v. State, 95 Wash. 2d 257, 623 P.2d 683 (1980).

[370] For a more in-depth discussion of the Albright decision, see Larry E. Ribstein, *Reverse Limited Liability and the Design of Business Associations*, 30 Del. J. Corp. L. 199 (2005); Thomas E. Rutledge and Thomas E. Geu, *The Albright Decision – Why an SMLLC is Not an Appropriate Asset Protection Vehicle*, 5 Business Entities 16 (2003).

[371] Albright at 544, fn 9.

assignee of a membership interest in an LLC may become a member only if all of the other members consent.

Much to the surprise and chagrin of the debtor-member, the court ruled that this statute did not prevent the seizure of the member's interest. It reasoned that in every LLC where there is only one member, the interest must be assignable, for the simple reason that there is no other member who can possibly object. Moreover, there is a rationale for the charging order limitation that is not present if there is only one member. If there is more than one member, permitting a creditor of one member to access the underlying assets of the LLC would disrupt the investment and the business of the innocent non-debtor members. The "compromise" is to permit the creditors of the debtor-member to access the distributions owing to the debtor-member, leaving the underlying assets undisturbed. But that rationale disappears if there are no "innocent" non-debtor members.

Florida's statute is distinguishable in one key respect. Florida has no provision similar to Corporations Code §17302(e) which explicitly makes the charging order the sole remedy. But California practitioners should not rely on this distinction. At the very least, every LLC should have more than one member.

In June of 2011, Nevada amended its charging order statute in response to the Olmstead decision to make it crystal-clear that a charging order is the exclusive remedy, even when the LLC has a single member.[372]

In a community property state like California, if an LLC has spouses as the only two members, and the interests in

---

[372] Nev. SB405, amending NRS Section 86.401.

the LLC are community property of the spouses, such an LLC would probably not enjoy the protection of a multi-member LLC. If either spouse is a debtor, then under the community property laws, the creditor will be able to charge the LLC interests of both spouses. This would mean that there would be no non-debtor members to protect with the charging order.

f. Reverse Piercing

Because of the charging order limitation, partnerships and LLCs afford a liability shield to its owners, by protecting (to some extent) the assets within these entities from personal liabilities of the owners. Similar to the traditional liability shield commonly associated with limited liability entities, the protection of the charging order may be pierced by a creditor. In that eventually the charging order limitation becomes a moot point, because the entity is no longer considered to have a separate legal identity from its owners.

In Litchfield Asset Management Corp. v. Howell,[373] after the judgment against her, the debtor set up two LLCs and contributed cash to the two LLCs. The LLCs never operated a business, never made distributions or paid salaries, and the debtor used the assets of the LLC to pay her personal expenses and to make interest-free loans to family

[373] 70 Conn. App. 133, 799 A.2d 298 (Conn. 2001). For a similar result, see C.F. Trust, Inc. v. First Flight Limited Partnership, 306 F. 3d 126 (4th Cir. 2002).

members.[374] The court found that the debtor used her control over the LLCs to perpetrate a wrong, disregarded corporate formalities and exceeded her management authority (in making interest-free loans), and ordered reverse piercing of the LLCs.

Because there has always been a strong presumption against piercing the corporate veil (including reverse piercing), this threat to the charging order protection should be easily avoidable.[375]

Practitioners using partnerships and LLCs to protect personal property, such as investment accounts and residencies should be wary. While most states allow the formation of partnerships and LLCs for any lawful purpose,[376] other states require a business purpose (profit or non-profit).[377] In a state requiring a business purpose, a partnership or an LLC holding personal property may be subject to a reverse piercing claim. Entities holding personal assets should be formed in states like Delaware, that allow entities to be formed for any lawful purpose.

g. Tax Consequences

The tax consequences of the charging order, to the creditor and to the debtor, vary before and after foreclosure.

---

[374] For a contrary holding, see 718 Arch St. Assoc. v. Blatstein, 192 F.3d 88 (3rd Cir. 1999), where the corporation paid personal expenses of the shareholder, but the shareholder included these payments as income on his tax return.

[375] Blatstein at 114.

[376] See, *e.g.*, Colorado Revised Statutes Section 7-80-103, Delaware Code Title 6, Section 18-106, Ohio Revised Code Section 1705.02.

[377] See, *e.g.*, California Corporations Code Section 17002(a).

Until the charging order is foreclosed upon, it is a lien on the debtor's transferable interest and can be compared to a garnishment. If the entity makes distributions to the creditor, then the tax consequences to the creditor are determined with reference to the underlying judgment.

The distributions made pursuant to a charging order are made in satisfaction of a judgment. Judgments are taxable based on the underlying cause of action, according to the "origin of the claim" test.[378] For example, if the judgment relates to a personal injury or sickness, it may be entirely exempt from income under Code Section 104(a). If the judgment does not relate to a personal injury or sickness, it will be taxable as either ordinary income or capital gain. Generally, recovery which compensates for harm to capital assets is a capital gain.[379] All other income is ordinary.[380]

While the creditor is being taxed on the distributions it receives, the debtor is also being taxed on the income of the entity. There are three ways to arrive at this conclusion. First, absent foreclosure, the debtor remains the owner of the economic interest in the entity. And whether the entity is taxed as a sole proprietorship, a partnership, or a corporation, it is the owner of the economic interest who is properly taxable.[381] Second, paying off the creditor reduces the outstanding liabilities of the debtor, which is an economic

---

378 U.S. v. Gilmore, 372 U.S. 39 (1963).

379 Rev. Rul. 74-251, 1974-1 C.B. 234.

380 Code Section 61(a).

381 Blair v. Comr., 300 U.S. 5 (1937) (gross income from property must be included in the gross income of the person who beneficially owns the property). Evans v. Comr., 447 F. 2d 547 (7th Cir. 1971) (the "real ownership" of the partnership interest was vested in the person who exercised dominion and control).

benefit to the creditor, and therefore taxable under the Haig-Simons definition of income.[382] Third, the charging order simply forces the debtor (to the extent it works) to pay off its debts. Paying off debts is not always deductible (see following paragraph), and changing the mechanism of debt payment (debtor paying creditor directly after getting taxed on its share of distributions, versus intercepting distributions from the entity) should not alter that result by giving the debtor an equivalent of a deduction.

The debtor may be able to obtain a deduction for any distributions made by the entity to the creditor, if the judgment relates to the debtor's business, and paying it off would be deemed an "ordinary and necessary" business expense.[383]

If there are no distributions being made to a creditor, then (absent foreclosure) the creditor is not taxable on the income of the entity.

Once a creditor forecloses on the partnership or membership interest, the charging order lien is converted into an actual economic interest in the entity, now owned by the creditor (or the buyer of the interest at a foreclosure sale). For federal tax purposes, the creditor acquires a property right in the economic interest (compared to the right to income), and is now treated as the owner of such interest.[384]

---

[382] Rutkin v. U.S., 343 U.S. 130, 137 (1952).
[383] Code Secton 162(a).
[384] Evans v. Comr; Rev. Rul. 77-137, 1977-1 C.B. 178. This Revenue Ruling ruled that an assignee that acquired "dominion and control" over the economic interest was to be taxed as a partner of the partnership.

The tax consequences to the creditor depend, on two factors, **(i)** whether distributions are being made, and **(ii)** the federal income tax treatment of the entity.

If distributions are being made, then if the entity is taxed as a sole proprietorship (because it is disregarded for tax purposes)[385] as a partnership, or a subchapter S corporation, both the debtor's share of the income of the entity and the character of the income being generated by the entity will pass through to the creditor. If the entity is a subchapter C corporation, its distributions will be taxed to the debtor as dividends.

If distributions are not being made to the creditor, then if the entity is taxed as a sole proprietorship, partnership, or subchapter S corporation, the creditor is still taxed on its share of the income of the entity, causing the creditor to generate phantom income.[386] The creditor will not be taxed on the income of the entity until it is distributed, if the entity is a subchapter C corporation.

---

[385] An entity may be disregarded for tax purposes if it is (i) a single-member LLC, (ii) either a limited partnership or an LLC owned by one person for tax purposes, or (iii) an LLC where only one member holds an economic interest and the rest possess only management rights. An example of a clause (ii) fact pattern is a limited partnership where individual A is the sole limited partner, and an LLC owned entirely by individual A and treated as a disregarded entity is the sole general partner.

[386] Pursuant to Code Section 61(a) if a sole proprietorship, Code Section 704(b) if a partnership, and Code Section 1366(a) if a subchapter S corporation.

h. Bankruptcy

When a partner or a member files for bankruptcy protection, the debtor's interest in the entity is transferred to his bankruptcy estate. The relevant question is whether the interest now owned by the bankruptcy estate includes the debtor's management rights, or solely his economic rights. Pursuant to the uniform acts and state statutes, the bankruptcy trustee should acquire the right to receive the debtor's share of distributions, but not his control over the entity. Bankruptcy laws may provide for a different answer.

Section 541(a) of the Bankruptcy Code provides that the bankruptcy estate will include all legal or equitable interests of the debtor in property. The courts are generally in agreement that Section 541(a) would apply to both economic rights and management rights of partners or members.[387] Section 541(c) provides further that no restriction on the transfer of any interest of a debtor (whether the restriction appears in a contract or under state law) prevents the interest from becoming property of the estate.[388]

Section 365(c) of the Bankruptcy Code provides, in turn, that if an executory contract contains transfer restrictions that are valid under state law, the trustee may not assume or assign such a contract. Consequently, if a partnership

---

[387] In re Garrison-Ashburn, L.C., 253 B.R. 700, 708 (Bankr. E.D. Va., 2000).

[388] Garrison-Ashburn at 708 ("Section 541(c) [of the Bankruptcy Code] makes plain that no restriction on the transfer of any interest of a debtor -- whether it arises from the operative documents themselves or from applicable nonbankruptcy law -- prevents an interest from becoming property of the estate").

agreement or an operating agreement constitutes an executory contract, then the restrictions on transferability of interests in such agreements would preclude the trustee from obtaining rights other than economic rights.

In determining whether a partnership or operating agreement is an executory contract, the court in Garrison-Ashburn concluded that the operating agreement was not an executory contract because it only established the management structure of the LLC, but did not create any duties of members to each other or to the LLC.[389] The court noted that in the operating agreement there "is no obligation to provide additional capital; no obligation to participate in management; and no obligation to provide any personal expertise or service to the company."[390]

It appears that in the context of bankruptcy, there is no clear cut answer whether the trustee (standing in the shoes of the creditors), will acquire solely the economic rights of the debtor, or the voting rights as well. If bankruptcy is contemplated, then the partnership agreement or the operating agreement should be drafted to impose various obligations on members—obligations to the entity and to each other. However, even if the contract is deemed to be executory, it is always possible to come across an "Albright"

---

[389] *Id.*

[390] *Id.* at 708-709. A similar conclusion was reached in In re Ehmann, 319 B.R. 200 (Bankr. D. Ariz. 2005). For a contrary holding, see, Broyhill v. De Luca, 194 B.R. 65 (Bankr. E.D. Va., 1996) (operating agreement called on the members to provide continuing personal services).

type court that will not even consider the executory nature of the contract.[391]

i. Maximizing the Utility of Charging Orders

Most partnership and operating agreements being drafted today provide that only the economic interest in the LLC may be assigned, but not the entire membership interest. This mirrors the uniform acts and the various state statutes.

A carefully drafted partnership or operating agreement can greatly enhance the charging order protection. As discussed above, the statutes allow partners and members to override the default statutory provision of assignability of interests. In most business dealings it would not be possible for practitioners to make LLC interests entirely non-assignable. Clients want to retain flexibility and ability to dispose of their LLC interests. However, in family settings, or for LLCs set up solely for liability protection purposes, it may be possible to either prevent assignability altogether or to limit it in such a manner so as to make the charging order remedy of little value to the creditor.

Because the charging order protection is predicated on the debtor's continued ability to manage the entity and thus control distributions, the distribution clauses of partnership/LLC agreements become critical. If the agreement provides that all distributions must be made to the part-

---

[391] For a more in-depth discussion of charging orders in the context of bankruptcy, see Thomas E. Geu and Thomas E. Rutledge, *Guess Who's Coming to Dinner?*, 7 No. 2 Business Entities 32 (2005).

ners/members on a pro-rata basis, then distributions have to be made either to all partners/members or none. This means that if one partner/member is pursued by a creditor holding a charging order, protecting that partner/member would mean withholding distributions from all other partners/members of that LLC. Consequently, agreements should be drafted to deal with this potential problem.

One possible solution is to allow the general partner or the manager, in the partnership or operating agreement, to make distributions to all other members, and not the debtor-member. The author's preferred solution is to provide that the debtor vests in the distribution (*i.e.*, cash and assets are distributable to the debtor) but instructing the general partner or the manager to withhold the distribution while the charging order is pending. This allows the entity to allocate taxable income to the creditor (following a foreclosure) without distributing cash to the creditor.

Pursuant to the uniform acts and most state statutes that allow foreclosure, prior to the foreclosure, the debtor may redeem its partnership/membership interest.[392] The statute does not specify that the interest must be redeemed for fair market value. This leaves room for drafters to insert various favorable redemption provisions into the operating agreement, such as a poison pill.

A poison pill provision usually allows either the entity itself or the non-debtor partners/members to buy out the debtor for a nominal amount of money. The poison pill has the effect of substituting the debtor's interest in the entity

---

[392] RUPA Section 504(c), ULLCA Section 504(c), ULPA Section 703(c).

with a nominal amount of cash, which limits the assets that a creditor can collect against. If the entity is established well in advance of any creditor challenges, when the partners/members do not know who will benefit from the poison pill and who will find it detrimental, it should be enforceable (although there are no cases on this point). Because the poison pill will kick in automatically, it should not be deemed a fraudulent transfer, although a challenge is likely. Poison pill provisions are usually limited to family-setting LLCs where the family members are on good terms with each other.

j. A Practical Take on Charging Orders

Charging orders generally allow debtors to retain control over partnerships and LLCs and determine the timing of any distributions. There are some exceptions to that general rule, particularly when the following facts are present: **(i)** there is a fraudulent transfer, and **(ii)** in the context of bankruptcy. It may be argued that single-member LLCs should also be deemed an exception to this general rule, based on the Albright case and the historical origin of charging orders. This author believes the Albright case to be an outlier, and in direct conflict with the charging order statutes of all states that have adopted single-member LLC provisions. Historical origin is also of little significance in this area. There is no need to interpret statutes that are very clearly drafted to apply to all LLCs.

Purchasing a foreclosed partnership interest may be foolhardy when the debtor, or a person friendly to the debtor, remains in control of the entity and can hold up the creditor's share of distributions. This will lead to adverse tax consequences for the creditor.

As a practical matter, creditors rarely chose to pursue charging orders.[393] A charging order is not a very effective debt collection tool. The creditor may find itself holding a charging order, without any ability to determine when the judgment will be paid off. Practitioners should remember that any uncertainty surrounding charging orders is uncertainty for both the debtor and the creditor. This uncertainty forces most creditors to settle the judgment with the debtor, on terms more acceptable to the debtor, rather than pursue the charging order remedy.

C. Creative Asset Protection Planning With LLCs

1. Series LLCs

Similar to corporations, LLCs generally protect owners from lawsuits directed against the entity. However, the assets within the entity are not protected from such lawsuits and the creditor of the LLC may be able to reach the entity's assets. Accordingly, instead of placing all assets in one LLC, practitioners advise clients to form multiple LLCs, placing a single asset in each LLC. At times, lenders also require borrowers to hold collateral in so-called special

[393] This conclusion is based on anecdotal evidence and the author's own experience. There are no available statistics.

purpose (bankruptcy remote) entities, with each entity holding a separate piece of collateral.

For a client who owns a couple of pieces of real estate (or other business assets), this structure works well. For a client with a multitude of assets, the fees (such as the minimum franchise tax imposed on each entity) and costs of setting up dozens of entities add up quickly. Series LLCs ("Series LLCs") are a creative solution.

The concept of the Series LLC has been adopted from the offshore mutual fund industry where segregated portfolio companies and protected cell companies have been in existence for quite some time. These concepts exist in such countries as Guernsey, British Virgin Islands, Bermuda, the Cayman Islands, Mauritius and Belize.

In the United States, the concept of a Series LLC was first introduced in Delaware in 1996.[394] The Delaware Series LLC statute was initially introduced for the mutual fund industry, as an extension of the series fund concept.[395]

Series LLC legislation has now been adopted in Oklahoma,[396] Iowa,[397] Illinois,[398] Utah,[399] Tennessee,[400] Nevada[401]and a few other states. All the states with a series LLC statute modeled their laws on the Delaware law, with some

---

[394] 6 Del. Code Section 18-215. It should be noted that Delaware also provides for series limited partnerships, 6 Del. Code Section 17-218(b), and series statutory trusts, 12 Del. Code Section 3804(a).

[395] The concept of a series fund dates back to the Investment Company Act of 1940.

[396] 18 Okla. Stat. Section 18-2054.4.

[397] Iowa Code Section 490A.305.

[398] 805 ILCS 180/37-40.

[399] Utah Code Ann. Section 48-2c-606.

[400] Tenn. Code Ann. Section 48-249-309.

[401] NRS Section 86.291.

deviations in the Illinois legislation (discussed below). Because most series statutes are similar to Delaware, Delaware series laws will be used to frame this analysis.

Title 18, Delaware Code, Section 18-215(a) provides:

> A limited liability company agreement may establish or provide for the establishment of 1 or more designated series of members, managers or limited liability company interests having separate rights, powers or duties with respect to specified property or obligations of the limited liability company or profits and losses associated with specified property or obligations, and any such series may have a separate business purpose or investment objective.

Section 18-215(b) provides:

> ...if separate and distinct records are maintained for any such series and the assets associated with any such series are held...and accounted for separately from the other assets of the limited liability company, or any other series thereof, and if the limited liability company agreement so provides, and if notice of the limitation on liabilities of a series as referenced in this subsection is set forth in the certificate of formation of the limited liability company, then the debts, liabilities, obligations and expenses incurred, contracted for or otherwise existing with respect to a particular series ***shall be enforceable against the assets of such series only***, and not

> against the assets of the limited liability company generally or any other series…[Emphasis added.]

Until recently, Delaware treated series as merely a bookkeeping concept, the series were not granted the power to sue, enter into contracts, etc.[402] Delaware legislature passed Senate Bill 96 that went into effect on August 1, 2007 and expanded the powers given to a series. For example, a series can now enter into contracts, hold title to assets, grant liens and security interests and sue or be sued.[403]

In several other respects, series are not treated by Delaware as separate entities. For example, series are not separately registered and they cannot merge or consolidate with other entities, convert into other entity types or domesticate to another jurisdiction. The Delaware Division of Corporations will not provide a separate certificate of good standing for each series.

Illinois has taken a much clearer stance on treating series as separate entities. Illinois law specifically states that a series of an LLC "shall be treated as a separate entity to the extent set forth in the articles of organization,"[404] and then also provides that each series may "in its own name, contract, hold title to assets, grant security interests, sue and be sued and otherwise conduct business and exercise the pow-

---

[402] See, e.g., H.R. 528, Section 9, 70 Del. Law Ch. 360 (1996) "a limited liability company may provide that such series shall be treated in many important respects **as if** the series were a separate limited liability company…" [Emphasis Added.]

[403] 6 Del. Code Section 18-215(c).

[404] 805 ILCS 180/37-40(b).

ers of a limited liability company…"[405] Illinois specifically requires that each series of an LLC be designated on the articles of organization and levies an additional $50 filing fee for each registered series.[406]

The other five states that have enacted series legislation do not treat series as separate entities and do not allow series to enter into contracts or sue or be sued.

Delaware further provides that to achieve the liability segregation that the series afford (the "internal shield"), the LLC must keep a separate set of books and records for each series, and to have a series enabling statement in its Certificate of Formation.

The following additional characteristics of a series LLC should be noted:

- **(i)** each series may have different members and managers, and the members of one series may have different rights, powers and duties from members of other series;
- **(ii)** each series may have a different business purpose or investment objective;
- **(iii)** statutory restrictions on distributions are applied separately to each series;[407]
- **(iv)** if a member redeems an interest in one series, he does not cease being a member of any other series;[408] and

---

[405] Id.
[406] 805 ILCS 180/50-10.
[407] 6 Del. Code Section 18-215(h).
[408] 6 Del. Code Section 18-215(i).

(v) a series may be terminated without dissolving the LLC.[409]

Series LLCs offer the advantages of cost savings and simplified administration. If an owner of multiple parcels of real estate can use one Series LLC instead of multiple LLCs, that allows for an effective reduction of filing fees, annual franchise taxes, legal fees connected to drafting operating agreements and possibly accounting fees. Because Series LLCs exist in a few states and there is no case law examining Series LLCs, several open questions remain as to their viability in other states. Here we will focus on the viability of a Series LLC in California.

a. Recognition of the Internal Shield by California

The major argument against the use of Series LLCs is the uncertainly of the recognition of the internal shield by a foreign state (like California) that does not have a Series LLC enabling statute. States that have enacted Series LLCs legislation usually expressly recognize the internal shield of Series LLCs formed in other states.[410]

If a Series LLC registers to do business in California or is involved in litigation in California, will a California court apply Delaware law and limit a creditor's ability to reach all of the assets of the LLC, or will the court apply California law and disregard the internal shield of the series? This

---

[409] 6 Del. Code Section 18-215(j).

[410] See, e.g., 6 Del. Code Section 19-215(m).

question is traditionally known as the "choice of law" analysis and has been codified in California, with respect to LLCs, in Corporations Code Section 17450(a).

Section 17450(a) provides that "the laws of the state…under which a foreign limited liability company is organized shall govern its organization and internal affairs and the liability and authority of its managers and members." The statute addresses two distinct sub-issues of choice of law: **(i)** when will California follow the laws of a foreign jurisdiction with respect to the internal affairs of an LLC (generally known as the "internal affairs" doctrine); and **(ii)** when will California follow the laws of a foreign jurisdiction with respect to holding managers and members personally liable.

The internal affairs doctrine has been interpreted to apply only to the internal affairs of a legal entity, its internal structure and workings, and should have no impact on anyone outside of the legal entity.[411] In a recent unpublished opinion, interpreting Cal. Corp. Code Section 17450(a), a federal district court concluded that the internal affairs doctrine, as codified in Section 17450(a), "does not apply to disputes that include people or entities that are not part of the LLC."[412] A similar conclusion was reached by another federal district court when it held that the internal affairs doctrine "recognizes that only one state should have the authority to regulate a[n LLC's] internal affairs. Different

---

[411] Bishop and Kleinberg, Limited Liability Companies: Tax and Business Law, 6.08[4] (WGL 2007), citing Restatement (2d) of Conflicts of Laws, Section 302, comment a (1971).
[412] Butler v. Adoption Media, LLC, Not Reported in F. Supp. 2d, 2005 WL 2077484 (N.D. Cal. 2005).

conflicts principles apply, however, where the rights of third parties external to the [LLC] are at issue."[413]

The second clause (governing liability of managers and members) is clearly inapplicable in a Series LLC analysis. With a Series LLC, the issue is not whether a plaintiff or a creditor can pierce the LLC and reach the personal assets of the member, but whether a creditor of an LLC should be limited to only some of the assets of the LLC because the rest are sequestered in separate series.

The above analysis of Section 17450(a) suggests that a Series LLC registered to do business in California would not be able to rely on the internal affairs doctrine to retain its internal liability shield in California. The analysis then necessarily reverts back to the traditional common law "choice of law" scrutiny which has been summarized as follows: "The local law of the state of incorporation will be applied unless application of the local law of some other state is required by reason of the overriding interest of that other state in the issue to be decided."[414]

California has never articulated an "overriding interest" or any other public policy grounds to disregard the internal shield of Series LLCs. That, however, does not mean that such an interest or a policy does not exist.

This determination will be made by the courts on a case by case basis. The court would weigh the injuries suffered by a California plaintiff, and how disregarding the internal shield would help remedy such injuries, against the inter-

---

[413] Chrysler Corp. V. Ford Motor Co., 972 F. Supp. 1097, 1103-1104 (E.D. Mich. 1997).

[414] Restatement (2d) of Conflicts of Laws Section 302, comment b (1971).

ests that members of other (non-debtor series) may have in the assets of the non-debtor series. It is possible to hypothesize a situation that would allow a California court to find an "overriding interest" in applying its own law.

Until this question is litigated in a California courtroom, the viability of Series LLCs for owning California assets or for transaction business in California will remain in question. However, if the choice is between using one LLC to own multiple properties and one Series LLC to own multiple properties, there is no disadvantage in using a Series LLC, and all of the possible liability segregation advantages of a series structure (if upheld in a California courtroom).

b. California Income Taxation

For income tax purposes, California Franchise Tax Board (the "FTB") piggy-backs its treatment of legal entities on the federal income tax rules.[415] Consequently, for income tax purposes California will treat each series as a separate taxpayer only if for federal income tax purposes each series should be treated as a separate taxpayer.

There are no federal cases or rulings dealing with income tax treatment of Series LLCs. The Treasury did issue proposed regulations on Series LLCs in September of 2010.[416] A series will be treated as a separate entity for federal tax purposes, as if it had its own juridical existence un-

---

[415] Rev. and Tax. Code Sections 23038(b)(2)(B)(ii) and (iii). See also Sections 17851 and 23800.5.
[416] 26 CFR Part 301.

der applicable local law. This means that while there is only one limited liability company that was chartered by a Secretary of State of Delaware, Illinois, Iowa, Nevada, Oklahoma, Tennessee, Texas, Utah or Puerto Rico, there are multiple entities for tax purposes.

Because each series will be treated as a separate entity, the traditional tax analysis will be applied to determine how such separate entity is treated for federal tax purposes. The analysis is completed under Treasury Regulations Section 301.7701-1(b). Thus, for example, if a series has one member it will be a disregarded entity, and if it has two members, it will be a partnership.

c. California Franchise Taxes

The FTB has issued instructions to Forms 568 and 3522 directing taxpayers to pay a separate $800 franchise tax for each series of an LLC.[417] Additionally, the FTB included more specific instructions in Publication 3556, Tax Information for Limited Liability Companies:

> For purposes of filing in California, each series within a Series LLC must file a separate Form 568, Limited Liability Company Return of Income, and pay its separate LLC annual tax and fee if it is registered or doing business in California, and both of the following apply:

---

[417] The $800 annual franchise tax is imposed under the authority of Rev. and Tax. Code Section 17941(a).

1. The holders of interest in each series are limited to the assets of that series upon redemption, liquidation, or termination, and may share in the income only of that series.

2. Under state law, the payment of the expenses, charges, and liabilities of each series is limited to assets of that series.

Note that Publication 3556 applies only if all of the requirements set above apply. The requirements are actually numerous: members are limited only to the assets of their respective series on a liquidating event, members may not share in the income of the other series, and the payment of expenses of each series is limited to the assets of that series. Many Series LLCs can be structured so as to fail one or several of the above requirements without sacrificing the internal shield.

For example, assume each series of a Series LLC is owned by brothers Abe and Ben. The LLC provides that Abe and Ben share in all of the income of all of the series and share in all of the assets of all of the series on liquidation. So long as Abe and Ben maintain separate books and records for each series, the internal shield survives intact (the separate books and records is the only mandatory requirement for the internal shield, all other provisions are discretionary). Consequently, Abe and Ben are not subject to multiple franchise taxes on their Series LLC.

It is also important to remember that the instructions in these forms merely express the FTB's position and are not a statement of the law. As the below analysis suggests, the position adopted by the FTB is devoid of any legal substance.

The FTB has not publicly disclosed the substance behind its position on Series LLCs. The author, over the past two years, has engaged in written correspondence with various FTB attorneys concerning the franchise tax treatment of Series LLCs. Based on that correspondence, the FTB's position is based on the following arguments:

> 1. For income tax purposes, series may be treated as separate tax entities (see discussion above).
> 2. A series of an LLC is treated as a separate "limited liability company" pursuant to Rev. and Tax. Code Section 17941(d).
> 3. Cal. Corp. Code Section 17450(a) does not apply to an LLC's classification for tax purposes.

Let us examine each of the points raised above. The FTB first argues that Rev. and Tax. Code Sections 23038(b)(2)(B)(ii) and (iii) mandates the classification of a business entity for California tax purposes to be in line with the federal entity classification rules. This argument makes no sense as the above Rev. and Tax. Code Sections deal with the classification of a business entity as a corporation v. a partnership v. a disregarded entity. These sections do not address whether a business entity exists in the first place.

The FTB then argues that because, for income tax purposes, each series may be treated as either a separate tax partnership or a separate corporation (see discussion above), California has the ability to subject each series to a separate franchise tax. This is a wishful leap of reasoning.

Rev. and Tax. Code Section 17941(a) authorizes the $800 on each limited liability company registered with the state. The statute specifically refers to a "limited liability company." There are no references to income tax partnerships, corporations, disregarded entities, etc. The only relevant test is whether a series is a "limited liability company." How it may be taxed for income tax purposes is entirely irrelevant.

To further illustrate this point, compare a series of an LLC to a general partnership. A general partnership is treated as a partnership for income tax purposes and is therefore an entity for income tax purposes. Yet, California does not impose a franchise tax on a general partnership, because it is not an entity chartered by any state.

That brings us to FTB's next contention: a series is a "limited liability company" for purposes of Section 17941(a).

California statutes define a "limited liability company" as an entity that is organized under the California limited liability company act,[418] and a "foreign limited liability company" is defined as an entity organized under the laws of a foreign state or country.[419] The statutes provide, further, that in order to form a limited liability company, articles of organization shall be filed with the Secretary of State. For franchise tax purposes specifically, a limited liability company is defined as an organization "that is formed

---

[418] Corp. Code Section 17001(t).
[419] Corp. Code Section 17001(q).

by one or more persons under the law of [California], any other country, or any other state, as a "limited liability company" and that is not taxable as a corporation for California tax purposes."[420]

If the FTB wants to argue that a series of an LLC is a separate limited liability company, then under the above test the series must be formed as a limited liability company. That is never the case.

A limited liability company cannot be created without the consent of a Secretary of State of some state. The existence of a limited liability company does not commence until the articles are filed and a charter is issued. Because no articles of organization are ever filed for a series of a limited liability company (with the exception of Illinois), a series of an LLC should never be a limited liability company under California law. None of the series jurisdictions include the series within the definition of a limited liability company.

The FTB concludes its arguments by claiming that Corp. Code Section 17450(a) does not apply to classifying an LLC for tax purposes. Which is certainly true. But Section 17450(a) does apply in determining how the state of organization treats the series of an LLC. If, for example, Delaware does not treat a series as a separate limited liability company, California should respect that treatment and under Rev. and Tax. Code Section 17941(d) cannot access the franchise tax.

While Section 17450 is discussed in more detail above, recall that this section forces California to respect the laws

---

[420] Rev. and Tax. Code Section 17941(d).

of a foreign jurisdiction with respect to the internal affairs of a legal entity. Pursuant to the internal affairs doctrine, the laws of the organizing state control the inner workings of a legal entity. Determining whether a legal entity constitutes one limited liability company or multiple appears to related to the legal entity's structure, and therefore its internal affairs.

In the case of a Series LLC, all the series comprise one limited liability company under the applicable enabling statutes, not multiple limited liability companies (again, with the exception of Illinois). Consequently, the FTB's position that each series is a separate limited liability company appears to be in conflict with the California statutes.

The FTB's position is further weakened in cases when the Series LLC owns only few assets in California and mostly transacts its business elsewhere. Assume an Iowa Series LLC has 50 series in existence. Forty-nine own real estate in France, and one owns a hot dog stand in Los Angeles. Because the hot dog series would not be able to obtain a certificate of good standing from Iowa, it would not be able to register with the California Secretary of State as a foreign entity. The Series LLC itself would need to register, and according to the FTB would then be liable for $40,000 of franchise taxes. This argument is likely to fail on constitutional grounds, but only if a taxpayer litigates. Until then, many taxpayers will continue to follow FTB's instructions and pay unwarranted franchise taxes.

Some commentators have suggested that the FTB's position with respect to the Series LLC franchise tax is not "completely objective."[421] This author believes that the FTB's position is so devoid of legal merit and is so self-serving so as to be shameful.

d. Recognition of the Internal Shield

The ability of a series of an LLC to seek bankruptcy protection is an unresolved question. Bankruptcy laws allow individuals, partnerships and corporations (and by extension, LLCs) to seek bankruptcy protection.[422] In series enabling states other than Illinois, series are not treated as separate entities (although Delaware comes close to that). Series appear to be nothing more than a bookkeeping concept, a virtual walled off part of an LLC. That may suggest that only the LLC can file for bankruptcy protection, not one of its series.

This analysis may be different in Illinois, where series are afforded the status of separate entities.

The next relevant question is whether a series of an LLC can transact business in another state without the LLC itself transacting business in such state. The answer to this question depends on whether a series is treated as a separate business entity. Under the Illinois series legislation, a series is expressly authorized to transact business on its own: "If a limited liability company with a series does not register to

---

[421] Bruce P. Ely and Kelly W. Smith, Series LLCs: Many State Tax Questions Are Raised but Few Answers Are Yet Available, Business Entities (WG&L), Jan/Feb 2007.

[422] 11 U.S.C. Section 109(a), ICLNDS Notes Acquisition, LLC, 259 B.R. 289, 292 (Bankr. N.D. Ohio 2001).

do business in a foreign jurisdiction for itself and certain of its series, a series of a limited liability company may itself register to do business as a limited liability company in the foreign jurisdiction in accordance with the laws of the foreign jurisdiction."[423] In Delaware and other similar Series LLC jurisdictions, series are not treated as separate business entities (although Delaware now allows each series to enter into contracts on its own), which would imply that a series on its own may not register in a foreign state.

Registration in a foreign state is available only to those entities that possess a charter (such as Articles of Organization) from their home state. While Illinois issues an equivalent of a charter to each series, Delaware and the other series states do not. Consequently, a series of a Delaware Series LLC would not be able to register with the State of California, the entire LLC would need to register.

Similarly, if one series of a Series LLC transacts business in a foreign state, would that mean that the foreign state would acquire jurisdiction and taxation powers over the entire LLC and all of its series or only those series transacting business? The answer again depends on whether the series is treated as a separate entity.

2. Use of Foreign LLCs

California law specifically provides that a foreign LLC registered to do business in California will continue to be governed by the laws of the foreign jurisdiction where it is

---

[423] 805 ILCS 180/37-40(n).

organized.[424] In this context, foreign means any jurisdiction other than California, including sister-states. That is why a Series LLC should work in California (noting, however, that a California court has yet to opine on Series LLCs).

Jurisdiction shopping for LLCs is relatively simple if one knows the client's objectives. For tax minimization, if the LLC is taxed as a partnership or a subchapter S corporation,[425] its state of formation is irrelevant to a member residing in California. California would tax any resident member on its allocable income. If the LLC is taxed as a subchapter C corporation, jurisdictions like Nevada or South Dakota (or even some foreign countries that do not impose an income tax) may be good choices because there are usually no corporate income taxes in these jurisdictions. However, this will work only if the business is either located in that jurisdiction[426] or it has no easily ascertainable physical location (such as Internet-based business).

For liability protection many look to jurisdictions like Delaware and Nevada, domestically, and such foreign jurisdictions as the Island of Nevis or St. Vincent and the Grenadines (both in the West Indies) that have an established history of making it difficult for creditors to pierce the corporate veil of an LLC.

Another advantage of using a truly foreign LLC for asset protection purposes is that the legal battle moves offshore.

---

[424] Corp. Code Section 17450(a).

[425] A limited liability company can file the IRS Form 8832 to elect to be taxed as a corporation, and then make a subchapter S election.

[426] If an entity is organized in Nevada (for instance), but is doing business in California, California will always tax that business on its income apportionable to California, regardless of the state of organization or type of entity.

With respect to LLCs, even if they hold U. S. real estate, the applicable law is always the law of the jurisdiction where the LLC is organized. Various offshore jurisdictions are more protective of LLC members than U. S. jurisdictions, such as restricting the creditors solely to the charging order, and respecting single-member LLCs as separate entities.

A foreign LLC also presents the creditor with the disadvantage of the increased costs of litigation, as the proceeding may have to be brought in a foreign country to either obtain a judgment or collect on a judgment.

Care should be exercised in the types of assets that the foreign LLC will own. For example, unless the foreign LLC is a single-member LLC and is disregarded for tax purposes, it cannot hold S corporation stock.

Clients often seek to protect corporate assets from creditor claims which may be prohibitive from a tax standpoint if the corporation is liquidated. Even with an S corporation, there will be an "exit" tax to the extent the corporation has appreciated assets. Transferring the stock of the corporation to a single-member LLC that is disregarded for tax purposes may be the best solution. Because there is some uncertainty as to how much protection domestic single-member LLCs afford, a foreign jurisdiction with a track record of respecting single-member LLC may be preferable.

3. Protection of Business Assets

Another way LLCs may be used to limit liability exposure is to form multiple (or series) LLCs to own separate, distinct portions of a business. If the business is held in one entity, all the assets of the business are exposed to risks and liabilities arising out of all the various business assets and operations. This is best illustrated by an example.

Tireco, Inc. owns a patent to an automobile tire and also manufactures and sells the tire. If a tire becomes defective and results in damage, the lawsuit will be filed against Tireco, as the manufacturer and seller of the tire. The lawsuit, assuming it is successful and exceeds the insurance coverage, would reach Tireco's assets (including the very valuable patent) and possibly place it in bankruptcy.

The solution is for Tireco to continue to manufacture and sell the tires but to form a separate LLC to own the patent, with a non-assignable licensing agreement between the two entities. If a lawsuit is filed against Tireco, the creditor would not be able to reach the patent. Note, however, that this protection may be undone by a successful alter ego challenge or "substantive consolidation" in a bankruptcy proceeding.

Any business with significant assets should consider forming a separate LLC for each distinct segment of its business or to hold valuable assets. Taken a step further, each significant asset of a business can be insulated using a Series LLC, with a separate licensing agreement (if appropriate) running from each series to the operating entity.

IX. Bankruptcy Planning

A. Overview of Bankruptcy Rules

In most asset protection cases, bankruptcy is the debtor's last line of defense. Regardless of all the other planning implemented by the debtor, without the debtor's ability to file for bankruptcy protection, the debt will always remain in existence. Once the creditor obtains a judgment, whether the debtor implemented a limited liability company, or a foreign trust, while the debt may go uncollected, the judgment will remain and the lien will continue to exist. Bankruptcy is the only way to permanently remove the judgment from the debtor's life.

To understand the protection afforded by bankruptcy and the planning involved, the practitioner must first understand some fundamentals of bankruptcy law, specifically as they relate to asset protection.

1. Property of the Bankruptcy Estate

Property of the bankruptcy estate is broadly defined in Section 541 of the Bankruptcy Code[427] ("BC"). It provides that the bankruptcy estate shall include the following:

a. <u>All interests in property except for assets in valid spendthrift trusts</u>. This includes all legal and

[427] Title 11 of U. S. C.

equitable interests the debtor possessed in property as of the date of the bankruptcy petition.

b. Debtor's interest in community property. All interest of the debtor and the debtor's spouse in community property as of the filing date, that is either: **(i)** under the sole, equal or joint management and control of the debtor, or **(ii)** is liable for an allowance claim against the debtor.

c. Fraudulent transfers. Property that was fraudulently conveyed by the debtor prior to bankruptcy and recovered by the trustee.

d. 180-day property. Any interest in property that **(i)** would have been property of the estate if the interest belonged to the debtor on the filing date, and **(ii)** the debtor acquires or becomes entitled to acquire such property within 180 days after the date of filing. This only applies to gifts, bequests, inheritance, property received under a divorce decree, or as a beneficiary of a life insurance policy.

e. Income, rents and revenue from property. However, debtor's post-petition earnings are not included in the estate.

f. Interest acquired after commencement of bankruptcy case.

Additionally, all powers other than powers that are exercisable solely for the benefit of an entity other than the debtor are property of the bankruptcy estate. Powers that are property of the estate are generally exercisable by the trustee. The following powers are included: **(i)** the power to revoke a trust; **(ii)** the right to disclaim property; **(iii)** tax elections; and **(iv)** certain other powers.

Only the property owned by the debtor is included. For example, if a debtor owns 99% of the stock of a corporation, only the stock is included in the bankruptcy estate, not the corporate assets. If the debtor holds legal title to property, but not beneficial, then only the value of the legal title is included. Additionally, the bankruptcy trustee cannot acquire rights in property that are great than the rights possessed by the debtor.

2. Fraudulent Transfers under the Bankruptcy Code

BC Section 548 is the federal counterpart to the state fraudulent transfer statutes. It provides for two types of fraudulent transfers (same as the states and the California law discussed above): actual intent to defraud, and constructive fraud based on insolvency. Good faith purchasers are protected just like under state law.

In the context of bankruptcy, the bankruptcy trustee may void a fraudulent transfer only if it was undertaken within two years of the filing of the bankruptcy petition.[428] This means that all pre-bankruptcy planning must be undertaken at least one year prior to the filing of the bankruptcy petition. If the debtor engages in a fraudulent transfer but later reverses the transfer prior to filing for bankruptcy, the earlier fraudulent transfer will be ignored.[429]

---

[428] 11 USC 548(a)(1).
[429] In re Adeeb, 787 F. 2d 1339 (9th Cir. 1986).

Because courts deal sharply with debtors engaging in fraudulent transfers it is important for debtors to complete all pre-bankruptcy planning transfers at least one year prior to the bankruptcy, and to fully disclose the transfers. An attempt to mislead the creditor or conceal a transfer from a creditor should lead to a denial of discharge. Once again, asset protection planning should not involve secretive or unethical conduct. If done right, asset protection should be open, ethical and legal, while remaining effective.

How does one distinguish between a fraudulent transfer and pre-bankruptcy planning? In an often cited decision a California bankruptcy court stated that:

> ...if the debtor has a particular creditor or series of creditors in mind and is trying to remove his assets from their reach, this would be grounds to deny the discharge. However, if the debtor is merely looking to his future well-being, the discharge will be granted.[430]

In the event of a fraudulent transfer within one year of the filing, not only will the transferred property be included in the bankruptcy estate, but also pursuant to BC Section 727(a) bankruptcy discharge may be denied altogether. Denial of discharge is a highly powerful weapon in the bankruptcy court's arsenal that is primarily designed to deal with pre-bankruptcy planning.

Generally, conversion of nonexempt assets into exempt assets on the eve of bankruptcy would not be indicia of

---

[430] In re Oberst, 91 B. R. 97 (Bankr. CD Cal. 1988).

fraud per se.[431] However, depending on the amount of the exemption and the circumstances surrounding the conversion, a court may find the conversion to be a fraudulent transfer. This is especially true when the conversion amounts to nothing more than a temporary arrangement. The cases that held a conversion of nonexempt into exempt assets to be a fraudulent transfer seem to focus on the existence of an independent reason for the conversion.

For example, if a debtor purchased a residence protected by a homestead exemption with the intent to reside in such residence, that would be an allowable conversion into nonexempt property. But where the debtor purchased the residence with all of her available funds, leaving no money to live off, that presumed that the conversion was temporary, indicating a fraudulent transfer.[432] Once again, the courts will look at the timing of the transfer as the most important factor. The further the transfer is removed from the bankruptcy, the better it looks to a court.

3. Exemption Planning

Despite the general rule that all property owned by the debtor is included in the bankruptcy estate, there are certain exceptions. The most important such exception is the exempt property. The purpose of bankruptcy is to allow the debtor a fresh start. To make the fresh start meaningful, the

---

[431] See, *e.g.*, In re Stern, 317 F. 3d 1111 (9th Cir. 2003). Retirement plans that were not exempt under ERISA converted to qualified plans fully exempt.
[432] In re Sholdan, 217 F. 3d 1006 (8th Cir. 2000).

debtor is often allowed to keep certain property (exempt property), such as tools of the trade, household furnishings, clothing, each up to a certain dollar limit. By exempting certain assets from inclusion in the bankruptcy estate the debtor is not left destitute.

All of the states have enacted legislation that sets forth the nature and the amounts of exempt property. The bankruptcy code also sets forth the federal exemptions.

BC Section 522 allows the debtor a choice—the debtor may either exempt from the bankruptcy estate the property listed under the bankruptcy code, or state exemptions. Certain states have opted out of the federal exemption scheme. In those states the debtor must use the state's exemptions and cannot use the federal bankruptcy exemptions. California is one of those states (California exemptions under CCP 704.010 and 703.140(b)(1)-(11), which would also apply to a California bankruptcy, are discussed above).

A debtor can use a state's exemptions if the debtor has been domiciled in that state for 180 days prior to the filing of the bankruptcy petition.[433]

B. Discharge of Debts

Not all debts are dischargeable in bankruptcy. Debts are not dischargeable if either: (i) the claim arose prior to the discharge, or (ii) they are specifically not dischargeable, such as certain taxes, alimony and education loans.

---

[433] BC Section 522(b)(2)(A).

1. Taxes

Taxes are dischargeable in only limited circumstances.

a. Income Taxes and Taxes on Gross Receipts

Three threshold tests must be satisfied.

First, the due date for filing of the tax return on which the tax was disclosed (including extensions) must have occurred more than 3 years prior to the bankruptcy.[434] Thus, for example, if a 2000 income tax return could have been extended until October 15, 2001, then the tax may be discharged if the bankruptcy petition is filed after October 15, 2004.

Second, the return must have been filed at least two years before the bankruptcy.[435] Thus, if the return due on October 15, 2001 was not actually filed under May 1, 2003, the tax will not be dischargeable unless the bankruptcy is filed after May 1, 2005. It is important for the debtor to verify that the return was properly filed and signed and is sufficiently complete to constitute a tax return. A substitute for return filed by the Service may not constitute a filed return.

Third, the taxing authority must have assessed the tax against the debtor at least 240 days prior to the bankruptcy.[436] The 240-day rule is tolled by: **(i)** the duration of each offer in compromise (that applied to the subject tax) plus 30

---

[434] BC Sections 532(a) and 507(a)(8)(A)(i).
[435] BC Section 523(a)(1)(B).
[436] BC Sections 523(a)(1)(A) and 507(a)(8)(A)(ii).

days, and **(ii)** the duration of each bankruptcy (that applied to the subject tax) plus six months.

If the debtor committed an act of fraud with respect to the subject return, or willfully attempted to evade the tax, the discharge of the tax will be denied.[437]

If a tax is dischargeable, then any penalties or interest related to the tax will be discharged as well.

b. Nondischargeable Taxes

The following taxes are not dischargeable: **(i)** the type of tax for which the debtor was responsible for collecting from the source and remitting to the taxing authority (*i.e.*, sales taxes, FICA, Medicare and other employment withholding taxes – trust fund taxes); and **(ii)** excise taxes.[438]

C. Preference Payments

1. Generally

The preference rules under the Bankruptcy Code allow payments of certain antecedent debts to be voided.[439] Subject to the exceptions discussed below, an avoidable preference payment is broadly defined as one that is **(i)** made to a creditor, **(ii)** with respect to an antecedent debt, **(iii)** while the debtor is insolvent, **(iv)** within ninety days before the date of filing the petition (or one year if the creditor is an

---

[437] BC Section 507(a)(8)(A)(iii).
[438] BC Sections 523(a)(1), 507(a)(8)(C) and (E).
[439] BC Section 547(c)(6).

insider), and **(v)** that allows a creditor to receive more than he would have otherwise received.[440] Under these rules a debtor is presumed to be insolvent on and during the ninety days preceding the filing of the bankruptcy petition.

The main purpose of the preference provisions is to prevent a creditors' race to the courthouse and thus ensure equality among them so that one creditor does not gain at the expense of others. Generally, any payment that reduces the debtor's bankruptcy estate, and confers on the creditor more than the creditor would have received through the bankruptcy is a potential preferential payment.

Any property that would otherwise be available to creditors can be drawn back into the bankruptcy estate as a preference, including, without limitation, property that has been fraudulently obtained by the debtor.

2. Exceptions

While all creditors are subject to the preference rules, there are certain exceptions designed to allow the debtor to continue its business prior to the filing for bankruptcy.

The exceptions include ordinary business transactions, payments in exchange for value, purchase money security interests and funds earmarked for specific debts.

An ordinary business transaction is the most common exception to the preference payment rules.[441] In order to qualify under this exception the transfer must meet three tests: **(i)** it must be incurred in the ordinary course of the

---

[440] BC Section 547(b).
[441] BC Section 547(c)(2).

business or financial affairs of the debtor and creditor; **(ii)** it must be made in the ordinary course of the business or financial affairs of the debtor and creditor; and **(iii)** it must be made according to ordinary business terms, for the relevant industry.

The first two elements are subjective tests that require an examination of the way the debtor and creditor regularly conduct business. The third element is an objective test that requires the payments to be based on standards prevailing in the particular industry

Other factors taken into account in determining whether payments are in the ordinary course of business include: **(i)** the timing of the payment; **(ii)** a change in the method of payment, such as by cashier's check rather than by corporate check; and **(iii)** payments made pursuant to unusual economic pressure and unusual debt collection or payment practices.

X. Retirement Plans

Planning for retirement plans is a challenging undertaking. Retirement plans provide owners with many advantages, including income tax, estate tax and asset protection. The income tax rules applicable to retirement plans, specifically the rules dealing with required minimum distributions, are very technical. The estate planning uses of retirement plans are also present, including the use of retirement plans to fund the bypass trust and to qualify for the marital deduction. These considerations are beyond the scope of this outline.

The asset protection advantages of retirement plans are the focus of the following discussion. Retirement plans present a major planning opportunity for asset protection purposes. Both federal and state laws favor retirement plans, and allow owners of such plans a certain sense of security with respect to the assets within the plan.

From an asset protection standpoint, retirement plans are broken down into two categories: qualified and nonqualified. This is the same distinction that is made for income tax purposes.

A. Qualified Plans

Qualified plans are a very important asset protection tool because such plans are required to include anti-alienation provisions pursuant to the Employee Retirement Income

Security Act of 1974[442] ("ERISA") and therefore are excluded from the debtor's bankruptcy estate. Commonly used plans which are protected by ERISA include defined benefit plans (like a pension plan), defined contribution plans (like a profit sharing plan), and plans to which employees make voluntary contributions (401(k) plans). Similarly, for a plan to be treated as "qualified" under the Code, it must contain anti-alienation provisions.[443]

Protection of ERISA is afforded to employees only and does not cover employers. The owner of a business is treated as an employer, even though he may also be an employee of the same business, as in a closely-held corporation. Accordingly, ERISA protection does not apply to sole proprietors, to one owner businesses, whether incorporated or unincorporated, and to partnerships, unless the plan covers employees other than the owners, partners and their spouses.[444] A sole proprietor can never be protected under ERISA (because you cannot be your own employee). For all other businesses where the owner is seeking ERISA protection, non-owner employees (other than spouses) should be added to the plan to maximize the plan's asset protection benefits.

---

[442] 29 U. S. C. Section 1056(d)(1).
[443] Code Section 401(a)(13).
[444] 29 C. F. R. Section 2510.3-3(b), 2510.3-3(c); Giardono v. Jones, 876 F. 2d 409 (7th Cir. 1989) (sole proprietor denied standing to bring ERISA action); Pecham v. Board of Trustees, Etc., 653 F. 2d 424, 427 (10th Cir. 1981) (sole proprietor is not eligible for protection under ERISA); In re Witwer, 148 B. R. 930, 938 (Bankr. C.D. Cal. 1992), aff'd, 163 B. R. 914 (9th Cir. BAP 1993) (debtor's interest in a qualified plan maintained by a corporation of which he was sole shareholder and employee was not protected by ERISA).

Section 541(c)(2) of the Bankruptcy Code provides an exclusion[445] from the debtor's estate of a beneficial interest in a trust that is subject to a restriction that is enforceable under "applicable nonbankruptcy law." The Supreme Court held that "applicable nonbankruptcy law" includes not only traditional spendthrift trusts, but all other laws, including ERISA provisions that require plans to include anti-alienation provisions.[446] Accordingly, all plans that are required to include anti-alienation provisions pursuant to ERISA are excluded from the debtor's bankruptcy estate.

Protection afforded by ERISA does not apply only in a bankruptcy setting. Even outside of bankruptcy, a creditor cannot reach the assets of an ERISA plan.[447]

Perhaps the most telling evidence of ERISA's protection is the Supreme Court's decision in Guidry v. Sheetmetal Pension Fund.[448] In Guidry a union official embezzled money from the union and transferred it to his union pension plan. The union official was convicted of the crime of embezzlement and the union attempted to recover the embezzled proceeds from the pension plan. Other than the fact that the proceeds were embezzled, the transfer to the pension plan was a fraudulent conveyance.

The Court held that the money in the pension plan could not be reached by creditors, whether by way of a constructive trust, writ of garnishment, or otherwise, because of

---

[445] An exclusion, as opposed to an exemption, is not limited in amount.
[446] Patterson v. Shumate, 112 S. Ct. 2242 (1992).
[447] Retirement Fund Trust of Plumbing v. FTB, 909 F. 2d 1266 (9th Cir. 1990) (attempts to seize plan benefits pursuant to state tax levy procedures are prohibited by ERISA's antialienation provisions).
[448] 493 U. S. 365 (1990).

ERISA's anti-alienation requirements. Prior to that, various courts and states carved out exceptions to ERISA's anti-alienation provision. The Court declared that exceptions to the anti-alienation rules were not justified by ERISA.[449] The protection afforded by ERISA's anti-alienation provisions applied regardless of how distasteful the debtor's behavior may have been or any applicable state public policy reasons (including a state's fraudulent transfer laws).

In response to Guidry and other cases like Guidry, Congress carved out several exceptions to the protection afforded by ERISA. These exceptions include: **(i)** a criminal violation of ERISA; **(ii)** a judgment, order, decree, or settlement agreement in connection with a violation of the fiduciary provisions of ERISA; or **(iii)** a settlement between the Secretary of Labor and the participant or settlement agreement between the Pension Benefit Guaranty Corporation and the participant in connection with a violation of ERISA's fiduciary duties. These exceptions obviously apply only to criminal conduct and only as such conduct relates specifically to an ERISA plan. Consequently, Guidry and its progeny continue to provide full protection to ERISA plans.

How important is it for a would-be debtor to keep money in a qualified plan? Certainly, at the time of a collection action, the debtor should have its money in a qualified plan. However, because the tax rules allow for such easy rollovers between qualified and nonqualified plans, in either di-

---

[449] However, the Court made it clear that the domestic relations and child support exceptions to the antialienation provisions of ERISA continued to apply.

rection,[450] and because ERISA trumps fraudulent transfer laws, debtors may keep their retirement funds in nonqualified plans. Prior to a creditor's collection action the debtor should roll the funds into a qualified plan.

It should be noted that ERISA's anti-alienation provisions do not apply to traditional support obligations for spouse and children. Also, under ERISA, retirement benefits can be divided pursuant to a qualified domestic relations order issued in connection with provision for child support, alimony payments, or marital property rights.[451] ERISA also does not protect monies distributed from the plan to the plan's beneficiaries.

The final exception to ERISA's protection are federal tax liens. There is no statutory exemption for ERISA plans from federal liens and levies, and the courts have held that the Service may collect against an ERISA plan.[452]

B. Nonqualified Plans

Nonqualified plans are generally not protected by ERISA, but may be protected by state statutes that exempt retirement plans from claims of creditors. The protection afforded by each state varies, based on the applicable statute and its interpretation by the courts.

For example, California protects "private retirement plans."[453] The California statute provides that private re-

---

[450] Code Section 408(d)(3)(a).
[451] Code Section 414(p); 29 U. S. C. Section 1056(d)(3).
[452] U. S. v. Sawaf, 74 F. 3d 119 (1996).
[453] CCP Section 704.115(a).

tirement plans are protected from creditors, both before and after distribution to the debtor, and defines private retirement plans to include: **(i)** private retirement plans (the California legislature has not fully mastered the art of defining a term); **(ii)** profit sharing plans; and **(iii)** IRAs and self-employed plans. Under California law plan assets continue to be exempt even following the distribution from the plan.[454] Similar to ERISA, an exception is carved out for child support obligations.

California's protection, although seemingly broad, is not without a limitation. The statute provides that for IRAs and self-employed plans' assets "are exempt only to the extent necessary to provide for the support of the judgment debtor when the judgment debtor retires and for the support of the spouse and dependents of the judgment debtor, taking into account all resources that are likely to be available for the support of the judgment debtor when the judgment debtor retires."[455]

What is reasonably necessary is determined on a case by case basis, and the courts will take into account other funds and income streams available to the beneficiary of the plan.[456] Debtors who are skilled, well-educated, and have

---

[454] CCP Section 704.115(d).

[455] CCP Section 704.115(e).

[456] In re Bernard, 40 F. 3d 1028, 1032–1033 (9th Cir. 1994) (annuity did not meet the reasonably necessary standard for an individual, age 60, who earns in excess of $200,000 a year, where he was also entitled to income from other sources upon retirement, including social security and pension benefits); In re Spenler, 212 B. R. 625 (9th Cir. BAP 1997) ($275,000 IRA was not "necessary" within the meaning of CCP Section 704.115(e) where 55-year-old physician who worked approximately 80-90 hours per week could save for his retirement out of his estimated $250,000 annual income).

time left until retirement are usually afforded little protection under the California statute, as the courts presume that such debtors will be able to provide for retirement.[457]

In California, the protection of a nonqualified plan focuses principally on defining the so-called "private retirement plan" and determining the amount that the debtor will need to have to provide for retirement needs.

The question of what constitutes a retirement plan was considered in Yaesu Electronics Corp. v. Tamura.[458] In that case the court held that the design and purpose of an IRS-qualified plan was not for retirement, since the debtor "admitted that he had never had a retirement account," and "conceded that his purpose in establishing the [Retirement] Plan was not to save money to use for his retirement but to take advantage of the tax laws and to save money for his children." Further, there was no evidence that the debtor used the money for retirement even though he was retired.

California courts have set forth several relevant factors to determine whether a nonqualified plan constitutes a "private retirement plan": **(i)** the purpose of any withdrawals from the retirement plan; **(ii)** whether the applicable procedures were followed, in this case for withdrawals; **(iii)** the frequency of withdrawals; **(iv)** whether the retirement plan was used to shield or hide funds from creditors or the bankruptcy court; **(v)** whether any withdrawals diminished or will diminish the assets to such an extent that they are in-

---

[457] In re Moffat, 119 B. R. 201 (9th Cir. BAP 1990), aff'd, 959 F2d 740 (9th Cir. 1992) (practicing orthodontist did not need annuity for support).

[458] 28 Cal. App. 4th 8, 33 Cal. Rptr. 2d 283 (1994).

consistent with the majority of the assets being used for long-term retirement purposes; and **(vi)** whether the debtor exercised such control over the plan so as to show a non-retirement purpose.[459]

Accordingly, while California does not provide for a clear cut definition, it appears that private retirement plans are broadly defined as plans intended to provide for the debtor's retirement.

Nonqualified plans garner additional protection from the fact that the underlying trust is often spendthrift in nature. Which means that the plan will contain its own anti-alienation provision. Thus, the Ninth Circuit held that the assets of a nonqualified plan were protected in bankruptcy under the California spendthrift statute due to the plan's spendthrift clause.[460]

While the spendthrift trust affords beneficiaries strong protection from creditors, it is subject to the prohibition against self-settled trusts. Because retirement plans are frequently established by employees for their own benefit, it would seem that the self-settled trust rules may apply.

In the Ninth Circuit, the prohibition against self-settled trusts has been modified so that such trusts have an enforceable spendthrift clause if: **(i)** the employer, rather than the participant, makes all contributions, even if such contributions result in a voluntary reduction of future wages, and **(ii)** the participant is not entitled to receive the contributions except indirectly as distributions from the retirement

---

[459] In re Anderson, 249 F. 3d 1170, 1176 (9th Cir. 2001); Schwartzman v. Wilshinsky, 50 Cal. App. 4th, 619, 629, 57 Cal. Rptr. 2d 790 (1996).
[460] In re Atwood, 259 B. R. 158, 161–162 (9th Cir. BAP 2001).

plan.[461] Thus, the less access the beneficiary has to plan assets, the more likely the plan will be treated as a valid spendthrift trust

In carving out this exception to the self-settled trust rules, Ninth Circuit noted the great value our society places on providing for retirement of individuals, and deemed that such value overrides the public policy reasons behind the self-settled trust rules.

It would appear that the protection carved out by the Ninth Circuit to spendthrift nonqualified plans would apply even to plans established by closely held businesses for the benefit of owner-employees, so long as the entity and not the owner-employee makes contributions to the plan.

Clients seeking protection for their retirement plans should always roll over their IRA to other types of plans. Additionally, converting to an ERISA qualified plans should also be considered, as ERISA plans are immune from fraudulent transfer challenges.

Frequently, financial advisors recommend to their client to roll their 401(k) and other ERISA-qualified plans into IRAs. In a recent decision, a California appellate court held that under the California tracing statute, monies rolled from a fully exempt retirement plan to an IRA remains fully exempt from creditor claims. The rollover is treated as just another distribution from a fully exempt plan and remains exempt so long as it is segregated from other assets.[462]

---

[461] In re Kincaid, 917 F. 2d 1168 (9th Cir. 1990).
[462] McMullen v. Haycock, -- Cal. Rptr. 3d – (Feb. 13, 2007).

ABOUT THE AUTHOR

Jacob Stein, Esq., LL.M.

Professional Biography

Klueger & Stein, LLP, 16000 Ventura Boulevard, Suite 1000
Encino, California 91436; Tel. 818-933-3838; Fax 818-933-3839
Email: **jacob@assetprotectioncalifornia.org**
Website: **www.assetprotectioncalifornia.org**

Jacob Stein is a partner with the law firm Klueger and Stein, LLP, in Los Angeles, California. The firm's practice is limited to asset protection and sophisticated domestic and international tax and business planning.

Jacob received his law degree from the University of Southern California, and his Master's of Law in Taxation from Georgetown University. Mr. Stein has been accredited by the State Bar of California as a Certified Tax Law Specialist, is AV-rated (highest possible rating) by Martindale-Hubbell and has been named "A Rising Star" by *Super-Lawyers* and the *Los Angeles Magazine* for the past several years.

On a daily basis Mr. Stein assists high net-worth individuals and successful businesses in protecting their assets from plaintiffs and creditors by focusing on properly structuring asset ownership and business structures and operations. Over the course of his career Mr. Stein has represented well over a thousand clients, including: officers and directors of Fortune 500 companies; celebrities; Internet entrepreneurs; high-profile real estate developers, builders and investors; physicians; wealthy foreigners; Ponzi-scheme investors; small business owners; attorneys, accountants and financial advisors; and many other individuals facing financial adversity or seeking privacy for their holdings.

Mr. Stein is an author of numerous tax and asset protection articles and technical manuals and a frequent lecturer to various attorney, CPA and other professional groups on topics ranging from asset protection to choice of entity planning, and offshore tax planning to advanced real estate exit strategies. Jacob is an instructor with the California CPA Education Foundation, National Business Institute and Lorman Education Services, where he teaches courses on advanced tax planning, asset protection and trust law. He is an adjunct professor of taxation at the CSU, Northridge Graduate Tax Program.

INDEX

H

I

J

L

M

N

O

P

Q

R

S

T

U

www.ingramcontent.com/pod-product-compliance
Lightning Source LLC
Chambersburg PA
CBHW060335200326
41519CB00011BA/1946

* 9 7 8 0 9 8 3 9 7 8 0 0 8 *